Dedication

This book is dedicated to my parents, John and Ruth Wong, who taught me the importance of valuing our differences. They also showed me by example the importance of never giving up -- even against seemingly impossible odds.

This book is also dedicated to the hundreds of new home salespeople, managers and construction workers who took the time to share their cultural insights and questions with me. In these pages I share some of those insights and attempt to answer many of those questions.

---Michael D. Lee

Acknowledgments

Our thanks to the following who helped make this book possible:

Production Coordinator: Donna M. Santoro
Cover Design: Group Two Advertising
Reviewer/Contributor: Marilyn McVay, MIRM, CSP
Project Editor: Jan Mitchell
Copy Editor: Lenore Cicchese

Other books by Michael Lee:

Opening Doors: Selling to Multicultural Real Estate Clients
© 1999, Published by Oakdale Press, Winchester, VA

D0188028

FOREWORD

By choosing this book, you are increasing your opportunity to learn more about your fellow men and women, their cultures and heritage and how that knowledge, effectively applied, can assist you in serving them better.

Because more than one million immigrants are purchasing homes annually (and that number is growing), The New Home Specialist Publishing Group is leading the home building industry with the latest information on multiculturalism from its resident expert, Michael Lee. Through years of study and personal experience, Michael has compiled the enclosed facts in such a way that you can apply this knowledge immediately.

New Home Specialist Inc., provides resources for superior sales and marketing strategies in the new home industry that are unparalleled. I have worked closely with its founder and president, Bob Schultz, shared the platform with New Home Specialist facilitators and invested time with their clients. I have discovered that The New Home Specialist's customized programs, systems, resources and mindset have always positioned the company and its clients on the cutting edge. This book by Michael Lee is no exception.

I wish you well on your road to MAXIMUM ACHIEVEMENT.

---Brian Tracy, Solana Beach, CA

When I travel across North America speaking to builders, salespeople, sales managers, Realtors and other home building industry professionals, I listen to what are some of their top concerns and priorities. Almost consistently, they tell me that they would like to know how to more quickly and effectively establish rapport with their customers, particularly as those customers are ever changing.

One of the challenges that we as home building professionals will face as we work in the new century is to reach the new profile of buyer. No longer is the typical American buyer a predominantly Caucasian family with roots in northern Europe. Depending on the part of the country in which you work, you'll be seeing a greater influx of newly arrived immigrants, as well as an increase in purchasing power of other multicultural buyers. In short, we had all better be prepared to meet, greet, properly communicate with and close these diverse groups of buyers.

The good news for clients of New Home Specialist is that we have an expert on multicultural relations as an integral part of our education and training systems. Michael Lee is that expert. He can teach us all how to best sell and market to people with many types of cultural backgrounds.

We are excited and honored to have Michael on our team at New Home Specialist and are looking forward to sharing his expertise with you.

CONTENTS

MAP OF THE WORLD:
PETERS PROJECTION:

World Map: Peters Projection. Copyright Akademische Verlagsanstalt. Produced with the support of the United Nations Development Programme through Friendship Press, NY. For maps and other related teaching materials, contact the Friendship Press agent: ODT, Inc., PO Box 134, Amherst, MA 01004, USA; (800) 736-1293; Fax: (413) 549-1293; E-mail: 0003475157@mcimail.com

This Map represents countries accurately according to their surface areas.

INTRODUCTION

**"Building Bridges" between the new home sales
professional and the multicultural buyer is critical
for success in the new millennium.**

Home building is big business – in fact, it's nearly a $200 billion dollar annual industry. However, without one million immigrants a year entering the country, home building starts would level off and begin to decline. Add to this over 70 million multicultural Americans who are already here, and you have a force that will impact home building for the foreseeable future.

New immigrants are especially important to home builders. Conversely, new homes are important to new immigrants. Nothing says more to friends and family that people from other countries have become a success in America than a brand new home.

Making the effort to learn about other cultures, customs and languages makes each of us better able to communicate. This kind of cultural exchange provides us with a round-the-world tour without the lost luggage, seasickness and expense. It can be a fascinating and enlightening trip for those who are ready and willing to take the first step.

This book is written to help anyone who is transacting real estate to effectively manage cultural differences. It has little or nothing to do with race, however. While the dominant racial group in the U.S. is European, there are significant differences between Americans of European heritage and recently arrived Europeans. An Asian whose family came here five or six generations ago to build the railroads that opened up the

American West acts more like a second generation Swede than a newly arrived Chinese immigrant. Hispanic Americans would readily tell you they have little in common with newly arrived people from Mexico.

THE MOST IMPORTANT RULE

Probably the most important rule in successful multicultural relations is: "Treat every customer as an individual." If you follow this rule, you won't make the mistake of mentioning your Japanese customers to your Chinese or Korean buyers.

Out of necessity, this book will make some broad generalizations about cultural "tendencies." However, readers are urged to realize that every customer, regardless of cultural background, is unique. Some of the people you will work with may not practice any of the beliefs outlined or may have an unexpected, unique personal set of traditions. The only way you can know for certain what beliefs your customer holds is by *asking*. This means taking an interest in your customers as individuals and genuinely desiring to know more about them, regardless of cultural background.

Chapter 1

THE DIVERSITY AMONG US

Massive immigration into the United States, the greatest part from Latin America, the Pacific Rim and the Middle East, is unprecedented in our history. In 1996, the United States Bureau of the Census reported that 21.8 million Americans aged 18 and over were foreign born. America allows more legal immigration than the rest of the world combined. Indeed, this influx will have such far reaching effects that the Census Bureau further predicts that 25% of all Americans will be Spanish-speaking by the turn of the century. In 1995, non-Hispanic whites accounted for 73.6% of the total population of the U.S. but will be only 52.8% by the year 2050.

New immigrants tend to live in large coastal cities when they first come to America. According to the Immigration and Naturalization Service, some 770,000 new arrivals settled in the gateway city of New York from 1990 to 1995. The 505,000 who came to Los Angeles made the second largest group to enter the country. The next largest destination was Chicago with 245,000, followed by Miami's 240,000, then Washington, DC with 199,500.

Fortunately for the building industry, these new arrivals exhibit a greater desire to own their own homes than the balance of the population. Statistics from the Federal National Mortgage Association (FNMA) promisingly indicate that immigrants who rent are three times as likely to consider buying a home as their number one priority as other Americans.

The numbers are even more startling in other areas. In Southern California, for example, 74% of Japanese Americans and 60% of Chinese Americans own their own homes. In line with that trend, 57% of Koreans and 33% of Vietnamese are homeowners. Thus, the coming decade will witness an immigration boom for those who have the necessary knowledge for success in this market.

The reason the term "multicultural" is used so commonly today is that new immigrants have their own cultures that they bring from their home countries in addition to adopting the culture of their new home, the United States. Nevertheless, they exhibit at least one characteristic of earlier arrivals to America, the willingness to save their money to reach their goals. Culturally diverse people also exhibit a special eagerness to work hard to turn their dreams of home ownership into a reality. The average American family puts away only two to four percent of its gross income in savings. Many new arrivals come with a long-held tradition of saving 25% or more of their income.

While a 40-hour workweek serves to satisfy most of us, our foreign-born counterparts commonly put in 60 to 80 hours. The most casual glance at these figures makes it clear: the combination of higher savings plus dedicated hard work and a greater desire to own real estate will make home ownership a near future reality for many, if not most, of this dedicated wave of new residents.

These facts foretell tremendous opportunity for new home builders and their sales professionals. People in the home construction industry can look forward to the benefits of doing business with new immigrant home buyers.

However, every culture is unique. Significant differences in language, dress, food, work habits and attitudes toward time can result in frustration for any American who isn't well prepared. Success in relationships with people from other cultures means you must learn the specialized ways of doing business with ethnically diverse customers.

Many new home sales professionals are frustrated by multicultural customers because they seem to follow an inconsistent and seemingly incomprehensible set of beliefs about which direction a home faces or the numbers in the address. Furthermore, they may appear to have an irresistible need to negotiate, a seemingly rude habit of talking in their native language in front of others, may continue to negotiate the terms of the purchase agreement after it has been signed, and so on. If any one of the above is the reason you purchased this book, then congratulations! It will help you to understand many of the different practices of other cultures and bridge the gap to building rapport and a rewarding lifetime relationship with your new home customers.

STEREOTYPES OF AMERICANS

Believe it or not, people outside the United States have stereotypical beliefs about Americans. True or false, these impressions affect their dealings with people here just as stereotypes of multicultural clients impact our dealings with them.

The first belief that others hold is that Americans are always in a hurry. As a result, they think we do not take the time to develop deep, meaningful relationships, and that we may also make rash decisions because of the pressure of time.

The second stereotype that outsiders sometime believe is that Americans only think in the short term. While relationships may last a lifetime in many other countries, they see American business and personal relationships continuing only for a few years. In fact, some believe that once a purchase agreement in the U.S. has been completed, that marks the end of business dealings. Sadly, this is too often the case.

The third stereotype about Americans is that we are somewhat brusque in our business dealings. This may be the result of our incessant need to "get down to business." Outside this country there is usually a lot more "small talk" before business is begun.

The fourth stereotype about Americans is that many of us are overly materialistic. Who could blame others for thinking this after seeing programs like "Lifestyles of the Rich and Famous?" Remember, just as we stereotype people from other cultures in our media, the media stereotypes Americans in other countries as being preoccupied with money, sex, violence and material objects.

The fifth stereotype is that we are very ethnocentric. Many of us believe that the American culture, the English language and the Christian religion are the most desirable ones. Others also see people in the U.S. as knowing or caring very little about world geography, culture or religion.

While these stereotypes are certainly not true of all Americans, I think we would agree that there are valid reasons others may draw these conclusions. Just as we would not like to be stereotyped, let us not be guilty of the same when it comes to people from other countries.

AMERICANS AND ASIANS: THE WIDEST GULF

Because of vastly different communication styles, Americans and Asians have the greatest potential for misunderstandings in real estate transactions. To illustrate, people acculturated in the United States give more importance to the speaker than to the listener. On the other hand, people from China, Japan and India view communication as a process of cooperation between the parties in which speaker and receiver work together toward eventual understanding.

Asians also have a different view of legal purchase agreements. Americans put everything they want in a purchase agreement. Signing it brings negotiations to an end, as well as their relationship with the other party, except for delivery of the promised goods. On the other hand, Asians put only the essentials into written agreements and leave the details for "later," which could turn out to be long after the actual written purchase agreement is signed, sealed, and delivered. For this group, signing a purchase agreement is just the beginning of a long relationship.

Some people in this country think that some practices common to Asian cultures are unethical. As an example, Americans believe that jobs should be given on merit. Confucian beliefs, however, lead some Asians to hire members of their own family over more qualified strangers, a practice which we disdainfully call nepotism. Indeed, given our cultural viewpoint, it is. By their beliefs, though, our practices are mistaken.

Americans believe in "speaking one's mind," while Asians believe that a show of emotion is neither acceptable nor well mannered. People here commonly express the wish to "know where they stand," whereas most Asians have learned to go out of their way to avoid confrontation.

Because of these differences and the beliefs that many Asians hold, this book will devote the largest amount of space helping real estate sales representatives and affiliated professionals understand their Asian clients. However, answers that may have eluded you about Hispanics, African Americans, Middle Easterners, Native Americans, Germans, French or others will also follow. If any questions remain, the final chapter will help you discover your own answers to everything you want to know about these clients.

Success with people from other cultures requires thinking of business relationships in a totally new way. Consider them partnerships in which you help your clients understand the real estate process and, in exchange, they teach you a little about their native language, culture and customs.

Most sales representatives simply ignore the fact that their clients are from another culture, and try to treat them like everyone else. While admirable, this ineffective tactic leads to miscommunication and frustration. Both you and your clients know you are different from each other. Trying to hide this obvious fact creates tension that can pervade an entire real estate transaction and prevent the rapport essential to success from developing.

Others protest that fairness compels them to treat everyone exactly the same. They are not concerned with the client's cultural background, they say, and don't understand why anyone would be. We can congratulate them on their attempt at impartiality, but the fact is they are missing the opportunity to fit their presentations and practices to the needs of special clients.

As you will see, there are important differences that your clients would prefer you not to ignore.

In fact, the law requires that you treat all clients fairly, not necessarily the same. For instance, would you treat a client with a hearing or sight impairment the same as everyone else? No, you would adapt to their needs. In the same way, we should customize each relationship to meet the unique needs of each person with whom we choose to work.

The successful sales representative acknowledges cultural differences and sets about to bridge the gulf by taking a genuine interest in the client's culture. People love to share their food, beliefs and language with those who show an interest. The result is that everyone wins. By helping to educate the sales representative as the sales representative does them, multicultural people take an active part in their own home purchase. This helps them feel much more comfortable with the process.

One barrier to understanding is that people in United States tend to see the world from the viewpoint of our unique American culture. In this country, as in others, most of us believe that our culture is the "best" culture and our way of doing things, the most effective. We trace our values, customs and beliefs back to the English common law, Protestant religious ideas, and a fiercely individualist American heritage. Americans believe that we alone are responsible for our own success or failure. But many other cultures steadfastly hold that a higher being is responsible for the bounty of life and that one must simply accept whatever it provides.

The religious beliefs of Asian immigrants run a complex gamut through Shinto, Buddhism, Taoism, Brahamanisn, Hinduism, and Confucianism, each possessing its own special point of view. Customary methods of negotiation are different, legal systems (or lack thereof) are diverse, and languages and accents are unlike what we are used to. Horror that it is to many Americans, they may value group success over individual achievement.

Another barrier to understanding between differing cultures is the impressions Americans develop from common media-borne stereotypes. Though usually unconscious and unwitting, many of these negative images can create confusion, even fear, in people who don't know they are fixed, and therefore suspicious, ideas.

Becoming more successful with immigrant cultures calls for setting aside those comfortable fixed ideas and opening up to other people's way of life. Pigeonholing and stereotyping others' beliefs and behavior in our own terms of what is correct or incorrect is counterproductive. While someone else's customs may be different to us, they are perfectly appropriate in another culture. Indeed, these practices may have meant the difference between success and failure or survival and starvation from thence they came.

Culture is acquired and learned through life experience; it influences one's outlook on life and other people. Race, on the other hand, is biological and has little genuine effect beyond one's appearance.

Even within the United States, numerous, distinct subcultures exist in the Southern, Eastern and Western states. Culturally sensitive real estate sales representatives know that it may be more comfortable to speak a bit more slowly than usual and be more relaxed in business manners in dealing with people from the South. Easterners generally feel more at home speaking quickly and getting down to business right away. Those who live in the West are used to easy, friendly mannerisms. Those who come from cultures outside this country seem to us to exhibit pronounced differences simply because we are not used to them.

To restate a vital point: The simple difference between race and culture is that culture is learned, while color is inherited. Most people would agree that African Americans, while racially similar to people in Africa, are vastly different in culture. Children of fifth and sixth generation families whose ancestors came from China, Sweden, or Patagonia are as American as baseball or apple pie. Looking different is not the test. (If there is a test to quantify all cultural differences, I haven't seen it, and I have looked!) The things that separate us are subtle and individual, but they definitely exist.

All that said, some will demand, "Cultural differences! What do you mean, cultural differences?" They assume that because we live in the same country we can't really be so different. And it's surely true in more ways than not. For a fact, we all think, behave and view the world from our own perspective. The longer a new immigrant lives in the United States, fewer cultural differences will be apparent, and they become more "mainstream."

GENERATIONAL DIFFERENCES

Generational differences are widely recognized, not just by sociologists, but by new immigrants themselves. The Chinese refer to themselves in terms of the length of time the family has been here. New immigrants are "first generation" and harbor the most unfamiliar beliefs and customs that may affect new home purchases. They are the least comfortable with American culture and language. As a result, many members of this group work long hours at menial jobs to survive and prosper. Their children, the second generation, learn to study hard in school to succeed in this country. The dark side of this admirable trait is that there is tremendous family and peer pressure to do well. The suicide rate among Asian school age children is alarmingly high.

The third generation of Chinese heritage retains little of the language skills and cultural awareness of their forebears, although their new home purchase can still be greatly affected by the beliefs of their parents and grandparents. It is a shame to lose one's cultural heritage in the proud Chinese culture. It is an even bigger shame to be unable to speak Chinese. In fact, the Chinese have a special term for those who cannot communicate in this proud language – *jook sing*, meaning "empty head."

The Japanese also specifically recognize generational differences. They call their first generation in this country *issei*, the second *nisei,* and the third *sansei*. In keeping with the simplicity of their traditions, these terms literally mean first, second and third. The three generations show virtually the same characteristics of change as the Chinese. So do Germans, Swiss, Italians, and nearly all new immigrants.

The generational difference is one of the reasons why there are so few minorities in the new home sales profession. First-generation Asians, for example, are very uncomfortable with the English language and American culture and so must rely primarily on manual labor to make a living here. The second generation gets an education and strives for "traditional jobs" where the path to success is well defined, such as in engineering, accounting, and medicine. The third generation and beyond are the first ones to consider nontraditional careers in sales and the arts, where success is not so clearly defined.

Almost all immigrant cultures are aware of these seemingly inescapable differences. You can always break the ice with multicultural customers by asking where their ancestors came from and how many generations have lived in the United States.

The second important step in breaking down cultural barriers is to know that the new immigrants cannot be easily lumped into neatly defined groups. Many Americans wrongly assume that all Asians belong to one big happy family with identical beliefs, languages, and customs. Since they look alike, they must be alike. Nothing could be further from the truth.

So, before we can proceed we need to look at the background of the various cultural groups.

THE UNITED STATES

United States is geographically the fourth largest country in the world behind Russia, Canada and China respectively and third largest in terms of population behind China and India. It is one of the youngest countries on the globe, being only a little over 200 years old. In contrast, many other cultures have been in existence for thousands of years.

There are approximately 270 million Americans, of whom 80 percent are comprised of people of Anglo-European descent. However, the ethnic composition of the U.S. is undergoing rapid change; that is one of the reasons for this book. African Americans currently make up the largest minority group, followed by Hispanics and Asians. The latter comprises the fastest growing minority group.

The United States was founded on Judeo-Christian principles and values. Most Anglo-European Americans are Protestants or Catholics. One of the major principles of these religions is individualism, where it is believed that we control our own futures. One of the popular sayings that reflect this belief is that "God only helps those who help themselves."

Americans value time as a scarce resource. Being punctual and prompt in both social and business settings is expected.

People in the United States are extremely competitive. Rewards are an important reflection of individual achievement.

Strong eye contact and handshakes are a sign of honesty and sincerity. Anything less is looked upon with great suspicion.

Americans have numerous superstitions such as: the number 13 is unlucky and black cats crossing one's path can bring bad luck, as can walking under a ladder. Good luck can be brought by the number seven, four-leaf clovers or a rabbit's foot.

People in the United States tend to associate the color white with happy events, such as weddings, and black with sad occasions like funerals. Red is the traditional color used for Valentine's Day and romance.

AFRICAN AMERICANS

African Americans are a distinct cultural group in America. They are a blended culture whose roots can be not only from Africa but also Egypt, Puerto Rico, Jamaica, Cuba, or any number of other countries. Anthropologists estimate that nearly 95 percent of African Americans are of mixed ancestry.

The Christian religion is an integral part of the life of many African Americans, most of whom are Baptist, Methodist or Episcopal. In fact, they account for the majority of Baptists in America and a substantial portion of Methodists in the United States. Music is also an important part of the culture.

At the time of the Civil War, 91% of the African Americans in the United States lived in the south. Since that time they have moved throughout the country.

Historically, African Americans have experienced widespread discrimination including segregation, absence of voting rights and refusal to sell or rent housing to them. This has resulted in the lowest rate of home ownership of any cultural group in the country.

There is a strong sense of pride in the African American heritage and in their cultural uniqueness. There is also a strong sense of loyalty to the extended family, which may include blood relatives and others upon whom the family can rely. This can certainly include real estate professionals.

African Americans tend to value the importance of family over individual success. It is expected that those individuals who do achieve success will share with the larger community.

African Americans tend to touch each other more than European Americans during conversation. Interrupting two people from this culture who are talking can be considered offensive. Outsiders can interpret conversations between two African Americans as being very dramatic because of the common use of large gestures.

Names given to African Americans are extremely important. Be sure to ask these customers what they would like to be called instead of assuming. Never call them by their first names without permission. African Americans usually do not make eye contact as closely when listening than when talking.

THE CARIBBEAN ISLANDS

The Caribbeans are a group of islands scattered across 100,000 square miles of the southwest Atlantic Ocean. It is a mixture of races, languages and cultures consisting of independent countries as well as territories. Languages spoken include English as well as Spanish, French and Dutch.

Jamaica is the Caribbean's third largest island with long beautiful beaches surrounded by lush green mountains ringed by cane fields, coconut and banana plantations. In this country that is about the size of Connecticut, tourism is the main industry. While English is commonly spoken, the Jamaicans also have a "pidgin" dialect known as "Patois" (pronounced *Pa-twa*), which is a mix of Creole English and West African.

There are two million Puerto Ricans in the United States, making up 10.5% of the Hispanic population in this country. This island nation was a Spanish colony for 400 years, and shortly after 1900 it became an American affiliate. Don't forget that its residents are American citizens, since it has been a U.S. Commonwealth for over 80 years.

In 1950 some Puerto Ricans began immigrating to this country. Their first stop was New York City, where most initially settled. Puerto Ricans have larger households than most families here, 37% of which are headed by women.

Today, there are over half-a-million people from the Dominican Republic in the United States. This island nation is only 15 minutes flying time from Puerto Rico, and Dominicans often have a close relationship with people from this neighboring island.

Cubans are the best-educated and most affluent Hispanic group, making up 4.7% of the Latino population. Most live in Florida and have come to the United States since 1960. Now there are over one million Cubans in America. So many Hispanics have settled in Miami, that police there tag the bodies of unidentified Hispanic men as "Juan Doe."

Other islands in the Caribbean include Aruba, the Bahamas, Barbados, the British Virgin Islands, Cancun, the Cayman Islands and Curacao.

Religious beliefs in the Caribbean range from old tribal religions with different degrees of Christian influence to purely Christian churches. In Haiti and the Dominican Republic, Voodoo is sometimes still practiced today. In Grenada, Trinidad and St. Lucia, religions can combine African and Catholic elements.

HISPANICS

There are around 40 million Hispanics living in the United States. The term *Hispanic* tends to refer to people who were born or whose background is from one of the Spanish-speaking Latin American countries, Spain or Mexico. People who come from Caribbean countries, such as Puerto Rico and Cuba, may also use the term.

"Hispanic" is not a race of people because most Hispanics are a mix of races. Most are "Mestizo" being of both Spanish and Indian backgrounds.

Some people from Spanish language backgrounds may not like the term "Hispanic" due to some negative stereotypes portrayed in the media. These individuals may prefer the term "Latino."

Many Hispanics are religious, primarily Catholic. For these people, the church and their beliefs play an important role in their lives.

Be aware that many Hispanics, particularly those of Mexican descent, have lived in the United States for several generations. These people may prefer to call themselves Americans as opposed to any other cultural-specific title.

The family is important to most Hispanics. The extended family also may include grandparents and godparents. The father is usually considered the head of the household, and he may make decisions around the purchase or sale of the home without consulting the wife.

Hispanics tend to be less individualistic and competitive than other Americans. They generally emphasize group cooperation and achievement.

This group may avoid eye contact as a sign of respect for authority. Gestures when talking may be broader than some people are comfortable with.

Time is more flexible among Hispanics than many other Americans. Appointments may not be kept as precisely as most people in the United States are accustomed to. The exception is people from the former British Honduras, now called Belize, who are usually very punctual.

Hispanics are the fastest growing group of minorities in America, but they are also not a homogenous people. The U.S. Census Bureau estimates that 22 million Hispanics in this country come from Mexico (61%). They have the lowest educational level of any minority group, with only 44% receiving high school diplomas and 6% earning college degrees. While schooling is important, family is a higher priority and it is the duty of older children to support the family, even if it means dropping out of school.

Mexican Americans tend to be fiercely proud of their cultural heritage, which is a combination of Spanish, Mayan and Aztec backgrounds. Their religious beliefs blend Catholicism with ancient Indian practices.

Some 12% of Hispanics are from Puerto Rico. Six percent of Latin Americans come from Central America, with half of these coming from El Salvador; twenty percent are from Guatemala and 15% hail from Nicaragua, while 5% of Latin Americans come from South America, with one-third of those from Colombia. The rest are from Ecuador, Peru, Argentina and Chile. Five percent of Hispanics come from Cuba and 4% percent hail from Spain.

There are over 1,500 different languages spoken in South America besides Spanish. Therefore, it would be a mistake to assume that just because someone is from that part of the world that they necessarily speak Spanish.

Remember, too, that when speaking about "North America," Mexico is also included in this geographic area.

ASIANS

While Asians comprise a relatively small proportion of the U.S. population (less than 5%), research puts their purchasing power somewhere between $100 and $188 billion. In addition, Asians have a particular desire to own homes far in excess of their statistical numbers. In some areas of the country, Asians are buying as much as one-quarter of the homes under contract at any one time.

Some of the Asian cultures are over 4,000 years old such as Chinese, Korean and Vietnamese. As a result, there tends to be a heavy emphasis on tradition and history. Learning something about Asian history goes a long way toward building rapport.

The family is extremely important to most Asians. This might include the extended family with several generations living in the same household. Elders are highly respected for their wisdom and knowledge.

Many Asians greatly respect education. They see it as a way to advance in this country. Asian parents may place a great deal of pressure on their children to do well in school. The suicide rate among Asian school-age children is high.

"Saving face," or avoiding embarrassment, is extremely important to many Asians. Some would rather die than lose face.

Direct eye contact may be considered rude or intrusive. Also, keeping one's composure is important because "control over the body is control over the mind."

Many Asians will ask what Americans may consider to be very personal questions when they first meet. Such queries as, "How old are you?", "Are you married?" or "How much do you earn?" are not intended to be offensive but are designed to determine the status of the person with whom they are talking.

Asians tend to be restrained in their public communications. Rarely is there any touching or use of large gestures when talking.

The 1990 Census shows that the majority of Asians in the United States were Chinese at 24%; Filipinos were the next largest at 28%. Southeast Asians, like Vietnamese, were 16%. Asian Indians and Koreans each represented 12% percent, and Pacific Islanders around 4%. It is predicted that immigration patterns will change these numbers making Filipinos the largest group, Chinese second and Vietnamese third at the turn of the century.

Unlike Caucasians, most Asians are usually quite adept at distinguishing between the facial characteristics of Koreans, Japanese, Chinese, Vietnamese, Hawaiians, Filipinos, etc. When the author was growing up, he learned very quickly that his parents did not want him to bring Japanese friends home because of the centuries-long animosity between the two cultures. Korea has also mistrusted the Japanese since Japan invaded that country in days gone by.

Even among the Chinese there are enormous differences in politics and economics. Mainland China, exclusively Socialist until very recently, is just beginning to make use of some capitalistic ideas. The island of Hong Kong, just off the coast of the mainland of China, is but slightly smaller than Los Angeles. Its bustling 6.3 million people are among the most entrepreneurial of Chinese anywhere in the world.

When the 99-year British lease on the island expired in 1997, the colony returned to Chinese ownership and control. As much as 20 years before the event, fear of coming effects caused many Hong Kong residents to sell their real estate holdings to invest in property in the United States. Seeming to validate their fears, the People's Republic of China wrote a new constitution before taking over, canceling many of Hong Kong's civil rights and most of its democratic laws. The huge buying spree of U.S. property has slowed only recently.

The larger island of Taiwan has 21 million Chinese people living under a more democratic regime, known as the Republic of China (ROC). Mainland China (PRC) has made threats to take over the country for years. It would be a gross error to confuse the ROC with the PRC in conversation with either nation's citizens because relations between the two incite much controversy.

Contrary to a common impression, Asian languages are vastly dissimilar. Koreans uniformly speak the Han'gul tongue, while the Chinese might speak any one of a hundred dialects. Although Chinese, Japanese and Korean writing appear similar, they are easily distinguished.

Many Asians practice Buddhism. In this religion the chances of having a higher station in the next life after reincarnation is determined by the number of good deeds done during the present life. There are two main types of Buddhism: "Theravata" Buddhism which is practiced mainly in Burma, Cambodia, Laos, Sri Lanka and Thailand; and "Mahayana" Buddhism followed by the inhabitants of China, Japan, Korea, Mongolia, Tibet and Vietnam.

Buddhism has also played a major role in the development of the culture of India for 15 centuries. In addition, Hinduism and Jainism are also important religions in this country. The majority of the over 500 million Hindus live in India. Closely related to the Hindu religion is the caste system that says that social status is determined at birth.

Buddhists believe in "Karma" in which your fate is determined by what happened in a previous life. This can cause some to be fatalistic when it comes to buying or selling a home.

Other Asians may follow Confucianism, which is very different from Buddhism. It emphasizes the welfare of the family over individual interests. It also stresses acceptance of authority. Mainly Asians in China, Japan and Vietnam practice Confucianism.

The primary religion of Japan is Shinto whose followers believe in "Kami." This is the power of nature that provides and protects its followers. Buddhism was introduced to this country in the 8th century.

The Philippine islands represent the only primarily Christian country in Southeast Asia being mostly Roman Catholic. Inhabitants there also practice Muslim as well as other religions.

PACIFIC ISLANDERS

The Pacific Islands are composed of three major areas: Polynesia, Micronesia and Melanesia. There are only around five million people in all of the Pacific Islands, but many are immigrating into the United States mainland.

Polynesia includes the islands of Hawaii, Samoa, Tahiti, New Zealand and Tonga. Most immigrants coming into America are currently from Hawaii, Samoa and Tonga. Don't forget that Hawaii is already part of the United States and people there refer to our part of the country as "The Mainland." There are 35,000 Samoans living in American Samoa and 65,000 living in the United States, including Hawaii. The people of the Hawaiian Islands have been heavily influenced by the Chinese, Japanese, Filipino and Korean cultures.

Melanesia includes the Solomons, Fiju, New Hebrides and New Caledonia islands. Micronesia encompasses the Guam, Mariana, Marshall, Palau, Caroline Gilbert, and Ellice islands. Guam is the most highly populated island in Micronesia, with over 90,000 people.

There are over 1,200 languages spoken in the Pacific Islands including Hawaiian, Samoan, Fijian and Tahitian. The religions in these islands can be just as diverse ranging from Christianity to Balinese and Javanese.

While 58% of the 365,000 Pacific Islanders here on the mainland come from Hawaii, about 17% have come from Samoa, and 14% are from Guam. Each has its own unique culture and language. Don't assume they are all the same.

Hawaiians' native language is a dialect derived from Tahitian and Polynesian languages, but the contrived dialect of "pidgin" is a combination of English and Hawaiian.

It is important to keep in mind that Hawaii has been a state since 1959. Therefore, using phrases like, "We in the United States," when speaking to these fellow Americans would be extremely culturally insensitive. Most Hawaiians are as proud to be Americans as anyone on the "mainland."

SOUTHEAST ASIANS

People in America tend to think of Southeast Asians as one homogeneous group. This is not at all the case. Vietnam is primarily an agricultural country with 55 million people. The early refugees in the 1960s were middle and upper class and had the financial resources to leave before the communist takeover. Today, more middle class Vietnamese are immigrating into the United States.

Laos is a small mountainous country of three million people in Southeast Asia. It is tucked between China, Burma, Vietnam, Thailand and Cambodia. Most of those coming to America today are Hmong (pronounced "Mong"), one of the largest hill tribes from the northern part of the country. They had a strictly oral form of communication, with no writing until missionaries introduced it to them in 1960. Many in this group have a strong belief in evil spirits.

There are around 160,000 Laotians living in the United States today. About one-third of those live in California. Many of the others live in Oregon or Minnesota.

Most Laotians were farmers living in remote villages. Living in America is quite a culture shock to this group, and many find it difficult to assimilate.

Cambodians are from a small agricultural country in Southeast Asia with seven million people. Most were farmers in their homeland with limited educational opportunities.

The majority of the people in Burma, Cambodia, Laos and Thailand practice Theravada Buddhism. There are also a number of people who practice Hinduism and Islam in these countries as well.

MIDDLE EASTERNERS

The Middle East encompasses a large area about the size of the United States and includes Israel, Iraq, Iran, Saudi Arabia, Jordan, Kuwait, Egypt, Turkey, Sudan and the United Arab Emirates.

The largest group in the Middle East is Arab. Most people immigrating to the United States are Arabs. There is also a large number of Iranians who fled the country during the revolution of the late 1970s.

People in Iran greet each other with a handshake and a slight bow. Most are devout Muslims and speak Farsi. Many people in the Middle East are extremely religious.

Saudi Arabians can greet each other with elaborate rituals. They may also give expensive gifts to real estate salespeople. This country is one of the most restrictive countries for women in the world.

The language most widely spoken in the Middle East is Arabic. It is the sixth most commonly spoken language in the world. Other common languages in the Middle East include Farsi, Turkish and Kurdish. The official language of Israel is Hebrew.

One would imagine that the Middle East presents a unified front to the world, but this is not the case. The Arab world contains 22 separate countries that have substantial disagreements ranging from economics to matters of religious interpretation. Iran, from where many of our newly immigrated real estate clients come, is not considered an Arab country because its people speak the Persian, or Farsi, language.

Nearly 20% of Arabs are Muslims who follow the religion of Islam. Islam is the second largest religion in the world. The largest Muslim country is Indonesia with large groups of followers in Asia and Africa.

Devout Muslims do not drink alcohol and may not eat beef. They are required by their religion to face Mecca and pray five times daily – at sunrise, three times during the day and at sunset. Muslims believe that Allah (their term for God) gave the rules for proper conduct in the sacred book of Islam, the Koran. While most Muslims do not believe in divorce, some may practice polygamy.

The Islam religion makes no distinction between religious life and all other facets of human activity.

NATIVE AMERICANS

Most of the two million Native Americans live in the western United States, with the highest concentrations in Arizona, New Mexico, Washington, Montana, South Dakota, North Dakota, Nebraska, and Kansas. Contrary to media stereotypes, only about 20% of American Indians live on reservations.

Many Native Americans do not believe in the private ownership of land. Many grew up in tribes or clans that consider themselves the caretakers of land, not the owners. Most have a great respect for the land.

Native Americans tend to experience contradictory feelings when it comes to investing in real estate. On the one hand, ancient Indian philosophy dictates that no one owns land, but rather simply uses it to sustain oneself without harming it. On the other hand, Indians know that American law encourages the private ownership of land. Native Americans have the lowest rate of home ownership of any minority group in the United States, at only 33%.

The family is more important to Native Americans than any material possession. Each family member is expected to support others in the family. They do not believe strongly in accepting help from outside the family.

Do not compliment Native American children as it draws harmful attention to them. They do not believe in standing out from the crowd and may even actively avoid competition. Harmony between individuals, society and nature is important.

Native Americans avoid direct eye contact as a sign of respect. They may take a long time before answering a question in order to give it the consideration it deserves.

Many people think Native Americans are passive because of their belief in "taking life as it comes." There can also be a great number of beliefs that can affect the purchase and sale of real estate. Much of this can relate to the harmonization of the home to the land. Also, certain pictures, dolls or animals may be believed to cause bad luck. The only way to know which they may be is to ask.

Religious beliefs of Native Americans can range from Roman Catholicism to traditional Indian beliefs. The Protestants also had an influence when they built missions on reservations.

One of the basic beliefs of Native Americans is the existence of two souls in every person. One is a "free soul" which is able to leave the body during dream-of-vision states. The other is a "life" soul that leaves the body permanently when the breath is gone.

In Alaska, there are three types of native peoples – Eskimos, Indians, and Aleuts. The Eskimo or Inuit settlements are scattered along the coast of the Bering Sea, on the Yukon delta, the Kuskokwim River, and Bristol Bay. The Indians settled along the rivers of central Alaska, as well as in the rain forests and along Prince William Sound. The Aleuts were maritime people who lived in the Aleutian Islands, the Alaska Peninsula, the Kodiak archipelago, the Pribilof Islands in the Bering Sea and along the Kenai Peninsula and Prince William Sound.

EUROPEANS

While currently not the largest immigrant group, Europeans from England, France, and Germany have had a significant impact on real estate in America for several decades. In fact, while the Japanese bought high profile office buildings in New York and Los Angeles during the 1970s and 1980s, the English actually were the largest foreign purchasers of American real estate.

Generally, Europeans are a visually oriented people (just think of the influence of the visual arts on Europe). If you have difficulty communicating with a European customer, try drawing a picture, which is much easier for them to grasp than verbal sales pitches. Europeans also tend to judge people by how they dress and the quality of brochures and other materials. Be sure to dress impeccably for this market, and use high-quality printing on any marketing materials aimed at this group. Remember, though the majority of people in the United States are of European descent, there are vast differences among the respective cultures.

The ideal English home is a house with a garden. The majority of people in England own a home, and densely populated condominiums, townhouses, or cooperatives tend to be the last choice in real estate.

Most people in France live in the urban areas so they are used to city living and are much more accepting than the English are of living in condominiums, townhouses, and cooperatives. Pets are extremely popular with the French.

The German people like investing in American real estate because it is relatively inexpensive compared to that in Germany. Land is at such a premium that many Germans will buy or rent small pieces of land for gardens.

Germans generally value orderliness, cleanliness and punctuality. If you really want to turn off potential German new home buyers, show up 15 minutes late wearing a wrinkled shirt and driving a dirty car.

CANADIANS

While Canada is our neighbor to the north, its culture can be as different as that of Asians. It's important not to assume that because Canada is so close that its people are the same as Americans.

In addition, laws are also different in Canada. For instance, there are no tax incentives to own homes in Canada like there are in the United States. Therefore, it's important to carefully explain the tax benefits of home ownership in America. It can substantially reduce the cost of owning a new home.

We will discuss some general characteristics of some, but not all, people from outside the United States and even multicultural Americans. You are encouraged to bear in mind that it is important to treat every potential client as an individual, just as you would like to be treated.

IT'S OK TO ASK...

Bob Schultz says in his best-selling book, *The Official Handbook for New Home Salespeople*, "Become a world champion at quickly establishing common ground with your customers. Do this by asking questions."

It's true. The easiest way to show an interest in your customer's cultural background is to ask, "Where are your ancestors from?" Notice that this question could be asked of some of Irish descent just as easily as Chinese, and with equally interesting results. If your neighborhood is in an area where there is a significant number of new immigrants, you will want to make this just as important a question as "Which model do you prefer?"

An interest in your customer's culture may teach you that certain colors carry special meanings that others may find quite incomprehensible. In Germany, red roses express love and romance. This would hardly be a fitting present for one's lawyer or mortgage lender in Germany, even if female. Here in America, red roses denote the same feelings in affectionate relationships, yet are acceptable in most other cases because they are beautiful and fragrant.

A person from some areas of Mexico could think himself insulted or even threatened by a gift in the color yellow because many people in that culture associate them with death. Traditional Chinese wear black at weddings and white at funerals, just the opposite of Americans.

Nearly everywhere, including America, numbers carry connotations of good or bad luck. We often hear people saying, "That's my lucky number!" Seven is often believed to bring good fortune in the West, while people from abroad cannot understand why buildings in the United States have no 13th floor. In much of Asia, the number four is thought a bad omen and the number eight lucky. In the face of this, woe to the new home salesperson who expects a newly arrived Asian family believing strongly in the science of numerology to acquire a new home with the address "4444 Fourth Street."

Notice that while other cultures have beliefs, so do Americans – they're just different. As you will see throughout this text, your new immigrant customers are not inscrutable or incomprehensible – just a little different. It is those differences that can be frustrating or fascinating depending on how you choose to approach it.

These bits of trivia about numerology and colors are certainly interesting, but have they anything to do with the building industry and related fields? Emphatically, "Yes!" Culture affects property transactions in more ways than the uninitiated American can imagine. No region of the country will remain unaffected by the historic influx of new arrivals. Everyone knows that the states of California and New York have historically had a high percentage of new immigrants because of the presence of the gateway cities of San Francisco, Los Angeles and New York. Surprisingly, some of the fastest growing multicultural populations are in North Carolina, Georgia and Florida.

Thus, no one in the real estate profession can expect to succeed in a multicultural marketplace without being aware of people from other cultures and intelligently putting that awareness to work. Consider the possible effects of rooms, a whole home and the overall appearance they give. Size, color, appointments, location and layout of the bathroom may be the deal maker or breaker for Hispanic buyers. Asian Indians much prefer large, formal dining rooms to the common American "dining area" or worse, the dinette. Many customers from the Middle East desire one-story homes. Such preferences as these may never be directly communicated, so if the salesperson is not aware at the outset, the customer might give up and go elsewhere without a word of explanation.

Home builders can use special amenities and color schemes to make their products attractive to particular markets. They can design floor plans to satisfy special cultural expectations. A thin line lies between the personal and the cultural; each assumes equal importance. As much may depend on what the customer is used to as upon what tradition dictates. The basis of many a traditional belief is lost in time. Few Americans know the history of our most common architectures, yet they usually have a preference for one or another kind. The same is true for non-Americans; they might not fully realize why, but they expect certain things in the homes they own.

Lenders who work with builders must be careful how they broach the subject of credit with new immigrants. The ability to buy on credit is not widely available outside North America and Europe. A number of cultures consider owing money a disgrace. In others, merely asking how much is available for the initial deposit could threaten the customer's life. Some ethnic groups pool their resources to help one another acquire property.

In more than a few places, banks are the subject of general

distrust.   This is so in countries where they have earned a
reputation   for   instability.   Not   every   government   protects
consumers through bank regulation. Worse yet, some bankers
have simply absconded with depositors' life savings.   These and
other issues may need to be addressed in the earliest stages of a
sales representative's relationship with new arrivals.

New   home   sales   professionals   must   understand   that
foreign nationals rarely recognize the profession we call a real
estate sales agent or sales representative.   The idea of a
professional whose job is seeking out prospective homes, showing
them to prospects and negotiating the conditions of purchase is
quite novel to most immigrants.   In some cultures, everything is
handled directly by the principals.   Others use lawyers for one
part, accountants for another, and the principals do the rest.   In
still other places, the buyer may have no part in the process until
time to write the check.   New home sales professionals must take
the time to explain exactly what they do, the benefits to the
customer, how they are paid, and most important, why this
laborious process is necessary in the first place.

Developers and salespeople must make themselves aware
of features that interest a certain group.   Many Asian cultures
have a preferred compass direction for the front door or attach
critical significance to the number of steps leading to the front
door or sleeping quarters.

Home builders can use special amenities, angles, and color
schemes to make their products more attractive to distinct kinds of
prospects.   They can design floor plans to please special cultural
expectations.

Straight lines are considered unlucky by the many Asians
who favor curved walkways, spiral staircases and round windows.

Hispanic buyers prefer stucco and rough-textured plaster to wood. Anyone who visits Mexico or our American Southwest will note the predominance of adobe buildings in those parts.

People from the Middle East have little interest in basements because they are rare in their part of the world, if they exist at all. It makes no sense to build a basement in sandy soil.

Developers and their salespeople who ignore cultural differences will waste a lot of time and could eventually and foolishly decide that it's simply not worth the trouble trying to deal with "unreasonable" people who see things from strange viewpoints. Those who take the time to educate themselves will be rewarded with increased sales and much smoother transactions.

Since the American history of placing great importance on the ownership of private property is not common to all lands, the mechanisms we use to protect it are not either. The developer that uses an escrow company and title insurance needs to explain the importance of these entities to new immigrants. Having one or both sides pay money to a neutral intermediary to collect the money, deeds and other necessary documents, see that the purchase agreements are adhered to, then transfer title, is confusing enough to Americans. If Americans sometimes think, "Here's another middleman who collects a fee without providing legitimate service," then it had better be carefully explained to people from lands with very different traditions. It would probably serve many salespeople well to become familiar with this necessary function.

More confusion ensues from the traditional Asian practice of seeming to negotiate endlessly after the purchase agreement is signed. An informed sales professional prepares for this common stumbling block by handling the problem solidly and firmly with the customer before it arises.

Obtaining inspections on such matters as pest control, roofs, and septic tanks can be another area impacted by culturally based misunderstandings. The services such companies perform are far less commonplace in the rest of the world. Hence, immigrant buyers may have trouble accepting that they are necessary. Often, professionals in these related fields become fodder for continued negotiation or are thought of as superfluous. If inspections are justified in a manner easily understood by the buyer at the signing of the purchase agreement, an excess of potential difficulties can be defused in advance. But as they are explained, it is vitally important to understand the point from which the customer views them.

The author no longer tries to count the number of times he has heard, "Why don't these people get it? They're in America. They ought to do as we do here!" This is particularly ironic because when people from this country travel abroad, we are often called "Ugly Americans." When Americans, with our 200-year-old-culture, travel to other countries many of us are offended to find that the people there don't speak English and behave like us.

It is even more difficult for immigrants whose cultures are thousands of years old to leave their behaviors and beliefs at home. No culture is universal, and few practices are common to all. Still, many immigrants struggle to adapt from cultural behavior developed over hundreds of lifetimes. Visit any English language adult course at night and you will see these people trying to learn the language and the America culture.

Plenty of people make a personal effort to deal equally with everyone. Admirable as this objective is, today treating everyone the same is not enough. To be successful with the tidal wave of new immigrants, we must be proactive and learn to appreciate and adapt to their way of thinking. This book is about those highly individual variations in viewing things in life that make us who we are and how they affect real estate transactions. More, it is about respecting the cultures of others and working harmoniously with people who don't always do things as we're used to.

Once the issue of culture is out into the open you can subtly move the conversation on the subject of their new home needs. As Bob Schultz says in his book, *The Official Handbook For New Home Salespeople,* "The better you become at asking questions and actively listening, the more often you can accomplish mutually satisfying objectives." Meeting all of the unique needs of our customers, regardless of culture, is the basis for providing exceptional customer satisfaction in the new home sales profession. By satisfying their needs, we will achieve the success we all aspire to.

"Each one of us is different... therefore we are the same."

Chapter 2

THE OPPORTUNITY

Between 1991 and 1996, 6.1 million immigrants entered the United States; by the year 2000 the tidal wave will have reached 10 million. This influx has fueled a boom in home ownership by people from other cultures. They hold better jobs than ever before and have more advanced degrees than in the past, giving them greater purchasing power than previous sojourners. As a result, minority households now account for nearly one-third of all new homeowners.

The most spectacular growth is in Hispanic households, which grew 16.3% from 1995 through 1997. At the time, according to the U.S. Census Report, residents from Mexico, Puerto Rico, Cuba, and South America numbered around 28 million. At the same time, other minority groups like African Americans and Asians also experienced substantial increases. From 1980 to 1990, for example, people of Asian and Pacific Island descent (Hawaiians, Samoans, Filipinos, etc.) increased their numbers from 3.8 million to over 7.3 million.

The main reason for the growth has been the increased immigration rate of these groups. It began in 1965 when the Immigration and Nationality Act replaced the restrictive national origins quota system. Since that time the trickle of new immigrants has expanded to become a flood of people from other countries seeking opportunity in America.

The one million immigrants who enter the United States every year will increase the minority portion of the American population from 24% in 1990 to 32% by 2010. Minorities will account for over 75% percent of total population growth during this time.

Immigration aside, another reason for the growth in home ownership by multicultural customers is their increasing birth rates. While the Caucasian population in America is expected to grow at a rate of less than one-quarter of 1% annually after the year 2000, different numbers are projected for minorities. The Census Bureau anticipates that minorities in America will grow by 74% from 1995 to 2010. The Caucasian population will grow by 26% in the same period. Latino immigration adds 325,000, with 550,000 Latino births adding up to a total of 900,000 for this cultural group alone each year.

As can be seen, immigrants are entering the country in record numbers. In 1996, 27.2% of the influx came from Mexico, 26.7% from Asia and 6.9% come from Europe. South and Central America account for another 11.9%, while 10.5% arrived from the Caribbean Islands.

Each state will be affected to a greater or lesser degree by this tidal wave. None will remain untouched. According to Census Bureau figures, some 9.6% of U.S. residents in 1997 were born outside of the country. This is the greatest number since 1930 when 11.6% of U.S. residents were natives of another country. At that time, the new arrivals were mostly from Europe.

The same Census Bureau figures show that California is attracting the majority, 24.9% of the state's residents being foreign born. New York is in second place with 19.6%, followed by Florida at 16.4%. New Jersey residents were 15.4% foreign - born. The Texas figure stood at 11.3%. Again, although most of these new Americans are from Latin America and Asia, every state is affected differently.

Even within a state there are marked differences in the make-up of immigrant groups. California's city of San Francisco attracts such huge numbers of Chinese that it now has the largest population of this Asian group outside of China. In Southern California, Hispanics from Mexico and Latin America predominate. Florida cities like Orlando draw Puerto Rican and Caribbean Island immigrants, while Miami attracts more Cubans because of its close proximity to that island country and its long established Cuban community.

In the Southern U.S. states, where many mistakenly think there is little cultural diversity, it is surprising to discover that groups like Asians are growing rapidly. By Census Bureau statistics, Asian population in the South rose 45% from 1990 to 1996. The largest increase unexpectedly took place in Georgia, where the Asian population exploded by 70%. North Carolina was next with a 62% increase. Florida experienced 57%, while Asians in Texas grew by 50%, and those in Tennessee soared to 49%.

These increases brought the number of Asians in the South to 1.67 million people. Compared to an overall Asian heritage growth of 45%, the population of African Americans in the South grew by 13%, and Caucasians' numbers rose by a comparatively low 8%.

No matter where you sell new homes, if you are in or near a major metropolitan city you will feel the impact of multicultural home buyers and sellers. Prepare yourself now for working with these new Americans, or you may have to find another line of work. However, remember that the forebears of many of the new immigrants have been in this country since its inception, or even before. The author is a fifth-generation Chinese American whose grandmother came into the world in Monterey, California in 1869.

Multicultural customers who are born in the United States should be treated just like any other American. Anything you wouldn't say to another American, you wouldn't say to an Asian American, African American, Hispanic American, Middle Eastern American, or any other. Saying, "You really speak English well" to any American whose family has been here for generations would be an obvious insult.

Consider the following story about Eleanor Roosevelt, who sat through an official luncheon next to a Chinese official she hadn't met. Although he was well dressed and obviously of some note, he never spoke, so the First Lady assumed his English must be poor. Finally, she thought to begin the conversation by talking about the meal, so the First Lady asked "Likee soupee?" The gentleman graciously nodded and smiled.

Minutes later, the same gentleman rose to give the keynote speech of the day in perfect English. Returning to his seat, China's Ambassador to the United States and graduate of Harvard Law School, Wellington Koo smiled broadly at the red-faced Mrs. Roosevelt and queried, "Likee speechee?" Readers are strongly advised to avoid such embarrassments.

So how do you know if your customers are new immigrants or natives of the United States? Just remember to ask, "Where are your ancestors from?" If the answer is Omaha or Topeka or San Francisco, you are obviously dealing with someone who didn't get here last year.

Again, remember that the longer an immigrant family resides in this country, the less strongly they tend to hold to the belief system of their mother country. However, cultural ties are incredibly strong and the author whose family has been in America for over five generations still exhibits a few of the traits of traditional Chinese.

While few African Americans are new immigrants, most consider themselves a distinct cultural group in the United States that has specific housing wants and needs. This group now numbers over 30 million, 12% of the total population. Of all the major cultural groups in America, African Americans have the lowest household income, due to various forms of discrimination that have been well documented. As a result, they have had the most difficulty in affording home ownership and only have a 45% rate of home ownership, compared to white Americans at nearly 70%. Only recently have significant numbers of this group been able to own property.

Because of the low home ownership rate of African Americans, new home sales professionals must spend a bit more time than usual explaining the process to members of this group. Not only is there a high probability they are first-time home buyers, but they may not have many friends or family who own homes from whom they can learn the procedure.

Native Americans are certainly not new to the United States and are a significant home buying force in many parts of the country. The two million members of this unique group are most prevalent in the states of Arizona, New Mexico, Washington, Montana, South Dakota, North Dakota, Nebraska and Kansas. While most Americans think that the original occupants of this country live on reservations, only 20% actually do.

Many people here also mistakenly believe that all Native Americans are alike. There are 308 sovereign nations across the

United States, each with their own territory, governmental structure and laws. The largest tribe is the Cherokee, numbering around 300,000. The Navajo are second in size, with the third largest being the Chippewa and Sioux with 100,000 each. There are also hundreds of tribes with less than 1,000 members.

As the above illustrates, every person is an individual regardless of cultural background. What is mentioned here as a cultural trait may not be so for your customers. Always treat customers as individuals, never assuming they will behave in certain ways or that they believe in any particular system of ideas. Use this book as a guide of some traits to look for and an explanation why some people do as they do.

This book intends to show as many of the ways people are similar as how we differ. We are made of the same material, have many of the same goals for happiness and fulfillment and have a natural human desire to avoid unpleasantness. Once we get past the differences, we can start to look for commonalties upon which to build a long-term relationship.

For instance, "ego" is an important fact of American culture, although it isn't ours exclusively. To us, it means pride or honor. The seemingly humble Asians have an ego as well, called "face." The Hispanic cultural equivalent is machismo. African Americans know it as "respect." Those from Jordan call it "pride." When selling new homes to these groups we must take this issue into account so they don't lose face, have their machismo offended, be "disrespected" or have their pride hurt.

Some aspects of culture are deeply rooted in the subconscious of most of us. Culture is a shared system of beliefs, values and customs that explain and simplify some of the basic aspects of living in society. It tells us how to behave and function within our own group. The danger comes into play when two cultures interact. Since they may see things in different lights, yet not understand the reasons behind the difference, there is potential for misunderstanding and conflict.

It's important to realize how we in the American culture view the world before we can relate to others. We prize individualism; the individual is supreme here. Most perceptions and value judgments proceed from that viewpoint. In other cultures, like Japan, Pakistan, Taiwan and Peru, group identity is most important.

We believe in equality of the sexes and express that belief in our laws and public policies. In other cultures, like those in the Middle East, women cannot vote or even ride in the cab of a truck with men. Americans admit to being materialistic and judging people by what they have, i.e., "keeping up with the Jones's." South American cultures believe in sharing material possessions for the benefit of all. We zealously compete for prizes and awards, while places like Japan emphasize harmony. Americans are somewhat future-oriented while those in the Philippines, Mexico and Latin American tend to live for today. At the other end of the spectrum, people in China and Japan place great stock in events from the past and the traditions that come from them.

Even the notion of "truth" differs between cultures. Most Americans believe "honesty is the best policy," while Hispanics may alter the facts slightly to save someone's feelings. The Japanese often nod their heads to say, "I hear what you are saying." Americans who interpret this gesture as agreement wonder why the Japanese seem to change their minds so often.

Working with multicultural customers is a tremendous opportunity to learn about other peoples and cultures around the world. However, you must be willing to expend the time and energy to do so, if you wish to become more successful in your new home sales career.

"People from other cultures want the same thing Americans want -- a nice home, a safe neighborhood and good schools for their children. "

Chapter 3

HOW PEOPLE FROM OTHER
CULTURES CHOOSE A SALESPERSON

As mentioned earlier, many multicultural new home buyers do not necessarily seek out a real estate professional from their own cultural background. In truth, few care about a salesperson's cultural group as much as they do care about trust, patience and personal interest. This is evidenced by the thousands of new home salespeople to whom the author has spoken who are totally baffled and befuddled by their multicultural customers.

Chinese customers often prefer a new home representative who is specifically not Chinese because they fear disclosure of personal financial information within their community. People of Brazilian heritage may not want a Brazilian salesperson because they want to avoid paying the high taxes imposed by that government. Toward that end, they prefer that their U.S. property dealings not be known. Although these concerns are generally groundless, a developer can do little to alter customer fears.

The average person in America thinks that new home salespeople are either simply order-takers or resale real estate agents who were not successful in selling used homes. While obviously not true, it means that new home sales professionals are subject to the same myths as are believed about resale agents.

A long-standing myth among Americans says that resale real estate agents and brokers do virtually nothing to earn ridiculously high incomes. The average person thinks that real estate professionals show a few homes, meander over to the close of escrow, and collect a big, fat check. They know nothing of the hundreds of actions required to successfully transfer property from seller to buyer. Such activities may include writing the purchase agreement, negotiating the purchase, and locating a suitable loan.

They also may have to conduct title searches, arrange for inspections and contracts for repairs of items disclosed by inspections, arrange for insurance, etc. Imagine the confusion of a person from a culture where few of these jobs are done by anyone.

Likewise, new home sales representatives should explain what they do for a living. Otherwise, just like they do with resale agents, buyers will ask for part of their commission, believing that they haven't earned it.

The following is a list of just some of the things that most new home salespeople do for a living. You may want to change or add specific duties you perform on behalf of your customers.

DUTIES PERFORMED BY
NEW HOME SALESPEOPLE

1. Provide brochures on available new home models.
2. Help buyer to know what questions to ask about new homes.
3. Explain the new home buying process to customer.
4. Involve the customer as much as possible in the new home buying process.
5. Explain the difference between production and custom builders.

6. Explain the benefits and drawbacks of production builders.

7. Explain the benefits and drawbacks of custom builders.

8. Provide background of builder.

9. Explain pricing policy of builder.

10. Explain powers and limitations of new home sales representatives.

11. Provide contiguous area map to customer.

12. Provide copies of reports hired by the builder.

13. Explain availability of local fire protection.

14. Explain initial deposit requirement.

15. Explain any additional investment required, if any.

16. Explain site selection process to customer.

17. Explain local zoning laws to customer.

18. Explain building code requirements to customer.

19. Explain surrounding land uses to customer and their impact.

20. Explain adjacent planned neighborhoods and their impact.

21. Provide customer with information on general market conditions.

22. Provide customer with information on specific real estate conditions.

23. Explain advantages and disadvantages of new homes vs. resale houses.

24. Explain advantages of energy-saving features.

25. Point out potential neighborhoods in the area.

26. Educate customer about ground movement issues.

27. Educate customer about flood issues, as applicable.

28. Educate customer about environmental hazard issues, as applicable.

29. Explain foundation types used by home builders.

30. Explain drainage issues, as applicable.

31. Explain wildlands issues, as applicable.

32. Explain the need for retaining walls, as applicable.

33. Explain fencing options, as applicable.

34. Explain mailbox requirements and restrictions, as applicable.

35. Explain any construction restrictions, as applicable.

36. Explain potential view restrictions, now and in the future, as applicable.

37. Educate customer about Agency laws and liabilities.

38. Explain the impact of other properties in the area.

39. Explain water bonds, as applicable.

40. Explain tax assessments specific to certain areas or regions as applicable in new neighborhoods to pay for schools, police and other infrastructure.

41. Explain school bonds, as applicable.

42. Explain geological reports, as applicable.

43. Explain topographical maps, as applicable.

44. Explain other disclosures from builder.

45. Explain impact of Homeowners Association, as applicable.

46. Explain homeowners Articles of Incorporation, as applicable.

47. Explain homeowners Bylaws, as applicable.

48. Explain how Homeowners Association's monthly maintenance investments are assessed, as applicable.

49. Explain how Homeowners Association budgets are prepared, as applicable.

50. Explain disbursement of Homeowners Association funds, as applicable.

51. Explain impact of Protective Covenants, or Neighborhood Guidelines, as applicable.

52. Explain Homeowner Association member rights to customer, as applicable.

53. Explain use of Homeowner Association common areas to customer, as applicable.

54. Explain sign restrictions to customer, as applicable.

55. Provide property tax information.

56. Explain the effect of easements, as applicable.

57. Schedule construction of customer's home.

58. Keep buyers informed about cutoff dates.

59. Assist customer in completing a Buyer Profile for the developer.

60. Write a legally binding purchase agreement with the builder.

61. Explain new home options.

62. Explain new home upgrades.

63. Educate customer about various floor plans available.

64. Show buyers how to decide on the most appropriate plan.

65. Show buyers how to look at new home models.

66. Explain construction terms.

67. Explain financing options.

68. Explain benefits of being pre-approved for a loan.

69. Explain how lenders qualify buyers.

70. Explain benefits of using a preferred lender, as applicable.

71. Explain architectural services, as applicable.

72. Show customer how to fit furniture into their new home.

73. Set appointments with design center.

74. Provide information on most appropriate plants and trees for your property.
75. Explain Final Report to customer.
76. Help the buyer understand that a new home will not necessarily be perfect.
77. Point out changes that could delay completion of the home.
78. Explain maintenance requirements of new homes.
79. Explain modifications that can be done at minimal cost.
80. Keep customer aware of cut-off date for grading.
81. Keep customer aware of cut-off date for foundation work.
82. Keep customer aware of cut-off date for plumbing.
83. Keep customer aware of cut-off date for framing.
84. Keep customer aware of cut-off date for room changes.
85. Keep customer aware of cut-off date for choosing accessories.
86. Explain pros and cons of electrical vs. gas service, where available.
87. Explain wiring options.
88. Explain electronics options.
89. Explain security options.
90. Explain cabinet options.
91. Explain flooring options.
92. Explain counter top options.
93. Explain roof options, where available.
94. Explain finishing options.
95. Explain exterior facade options, where available.
96. Explain landscape options, where available.
97. Explain color options.
98. Explain carpet options.

99. Explain air conditioning option, as applicable.

100. Conduct final new home orientation of the completed home.

101. Explain options for selling an existing residence.

102. Order electric service.

103. Stay in constant contact with customer during construction period.

104. Explain Builder's Disclosure to customer.

105. Explain impact of changes in purchase agreement made by builder.

106. Explain impact of changes in purchase agreement made by customer.

107. Explain any addenda to the purchase agreement.

108. Explain any contingencies placed in the purchase agreement by builder.

109. Explain any contingencies placed in the purchase agreement by customer.

110. Explain warranty protection provided by builder.

111. Explain warranty protection of appliances provided by manufacturers.

112. Explain warranty protection of roof provided by installer.

113. Provide information to customer on schools in the area.

114. Provide information to customer on local shopping areas.

115. Provide information to customer on nearby parks and recreation areas.

116. Constantly maintain knowledge of home inventory.

117. Constantly maintain knowledge of real estate laws affecting new homes.

118. Constantly maintain knowledge of economic factors affecting new homes.

119. Explain insurance requirements to customer.
120. Explain final walk-through or "new home orientation" procedure to customer.
121. Explain proper maintenance of heating and air conditioning system, as applicable.
122. Explain proper maintenance of appliances.
123. Explain proper maintenance of foundation and drainage.
124. Explain proper maintenance of electrical system.
125. Explain proper maintenance of plumbing system.
126. Explain proper maintenance of landscaping.
127. Explain proper maintenance of roof.
128. Explain proper maintenance of exterior.
129. Explain procedure for handling system emergencies.
130. Refer customer to a selling agent to help selling existing home, as applicable.
131. Refer customers to a more appropriate neighborhood if you can't meet their needs.
132. Maintain a high standard of ethical practice.

Resale real estate professionals face a second myth about the amount and source of their compensation. Some people believe that sales representatives receive a salary from the company. Others believe that all sales representatives receive a part of the commission from any transaction that goes through the office or an office with the same name (if a franchise). Most people in America think that the sales representative takes home around 6% percent of the sales price.

The resale professional sales agent knows that nothing is farther from the truth. First, when working with buyers from a different company, the listing agent, usually represents the seller.

It takes about half the commission, leaving the selling agent with only 3%. But this is not take-home pay which customers understand. The agent's broker has rent, utilities, telephone and advertising for which it expects reimbursement from the agent. Those costs absorb about 1/3 of the commission, leaving the selling agent with perhaps 2%.

But this is still not the agent's take-home pay, since he or she must still cover his or her own necessary expenses to earn a commission. These costs include professional liability insurance, multiple listing fees, gasoline and automobile insurance, computers, phones, cellular phones, income taxes and more, finally leave the selling agent with a net commission of perhaps 1% of the original 6% or less.

Again, this misconception affects sales representatives who work for builders because this 6% is what people think they get for selling a new home. It's important to explain how much you earn from the sale of a home; otherwise buyers will demand some of this exorbitant fee. However, remember to explain your commission in terms of take-home pay but deducting income taxes (around 50%) and any other expenses. This leaves the average commissioned new home salesperson with around ½ of 1% to feed his or her family, pay for the family home and put children through school.

Many salespeople are reluctant to discuss how much commission they make, but if you don't, the customer is already assuming you get 6% or more. If you fail to explain how much you make and all of the services you provide to earn it, don't be surprised if your commission becomes an integral part of the negotiations of a new home.

With these persistent myths so common among

Americans, imagine what people from other countries must think! Obviously, it is doubly important that salespeople explain their duties and compensation to every customer. This should be done as soon as possible after rapport is established.

Few people from immigrant cultures care about a new home salesperson's experience or the number of homes he or she has closed. Customers only care about one home - theirs. People who are new to this country are concerned to a much greater degree that the sales representative is honest and trustworthy than they do about professional awards and applause. The fact that you are a good parent is far more important to them than being "Salesperson of the Month or even of the year, for that matter. Likewise, the belief that you care more about them than you do about your commission outweighs all the professional recognition you have ever received.

Stories about times when you demonstrated these qualities should be told during the rapport-building stage. Many cultures transmit information from one generation to another through storytelling, called oral tradition, and truly appreciate a salesperson who uses this method to communicate. This is far more effective with multicultural people than a canned sales pitch.

Filipino customers may prefer an "American sales representative" for other reasons. Since the United States ruled their homeland for five decades after 1898, some Filipinos have great appreciation for everything American out of a belief that they are probably worthy and reliable.

Filipinos may trust and believe Americans more than their own cultural brethren. The mistrust some Filipinos have for agents from their own culture comes from the Philippine practice of *la gai* or "grease money." Much business is done in the Philippines through *la gai*. For instance, a sales representative there who refers a roofer or contractor to a customer expects *la gai* in return from the service provider. This practice drives up the cost of a new home in direct proportion to the number of people involved.

La gai can affect a new home purchase if the salesperson fails to teach Filipino customers early how hard they work and how little they really earn. Customers may expect *la gai* from a representative who hasn't informed them on such issues. The customer may feel that a sales representative from his own culture receives *la gai* from contractors or the builder, driving the price higher. They may even believe that using an American salesperson will make the purchase price lower in the absence of *la gai*. In addition, Filipinos may expect representatives to continue to serve them long after the transaction is complete. It's not unusual to ask their salesperson to help locate a roofer, electrician or even someone to help them clean the home years after the close of escrow. If they were never informed, they may think that since you are getting *la gai* from other service providers you should give them some help in exchange. So, it's important if you are on commission to explain that all your pay comes from the one transaction. Tell them that you will be happy to refer them to appropriate professionals, but can do no more than that.

La gai is similar to the practice known as *sogok* in Indonesia. This term also translates as "grease money." Educate these customers the same as Filipinos. Explain to them how hard you work for how little money. If you do, demands for *sogok* are less likely.

In China, there is the practice of *guanxi* (pronounced *gwan-shee*). This is sometimes considered bribery as well, but is more of a referral network to locate a trustworthy builder.

Similar systems of "greasing the skids" are common all around the world. In Mexico, petty official bribery is known as *la mordida*. The Arab world knows it as *baksheesh*. Immigrants from these and other areas come with the expectation of having to deal with it everywhere they go. Most are surprised, and many disbelieving, when they learn that such practices are condemned as unethical here.

There is no question that customers want to trust the builder and salesperson of the new home they are buying. In the best case, you are referred from and introduced by a satisfied customer of the same culture. Referrals from real estate agents are almost as good. Either gives you credibility at the outset. After the introduction, you can help yourself by sharing stories from your personal life, demonstrating the highly valued qualities of openness and honesty.

African Americans present a contradiction when they choose a sales representative. Until passage of the Civil Rights Act of 1964, there was only limited contact between this group and Caucasians. Many believe racism causes the economic gulf between themselves and the dominant culture. This belief helps perpetuate the ill feelings some African Americans harbor toward members of the Caucasian race. Buyers who feel this way may feel more comfortable looking to salespeople from their own culture first. At the same time, other African Americans have for some time seen anything from the dominant culture as superior to their own. This misconception may cause them deliberately to seek a Caucasian builder representative. It's important that non-

African American new home salespeople realize that this confusing dynamic exists and be prepared to deal with it.

Americans who are most credible in business demonstrate decisive, unyielding and confident behavior. The opposite is true in other cultures. Well regarded Japanese leaders take great pains to appear indirect, flexible and humble. It would serve salespeople well when dealing with customers from this culture to take a similar approach. At the other extreme, Middle Eastern men may expect a new home representative to tell them how great they are. Bragging in this culture has been elevated to a high art, and people are expected to "toot their own horn."

Some Hispanics come from countries where education is not highly valued. Those who come here for purely economic reasons are, in general, not as well schooled as those whose driving purpose in immigrating is education. In proof, the literacy rate of Mexico is one of the lowest in the world. Having little familiarity with the value of education, their vision of the American opportunity may encompass little more than respectable housing and a well-paying job.

This lack of schooling on the part of some Hispanics means that a good new home salesperson will carefully and patiently explain such foreign concepts as construction, the home buying process and financing, then answer every question until the new ideas are clearly understood. As noted earlier, 70% of White households own a home, while only 44% of Hispanics are so fortunate. As with African Americans, they may know few people who own property from whom they could learn this complex subject.

Understand at all times that lack of knowledge is not the same as stupidity. Demonstrate respect and go out of your way to do your job conscientiously, and the Hispanic customer will be quite loyal and may provide you many enthusiastic referrals.

At the other end of the academic spectrum, educated Latin Americans and Japanese often put titles and degrees on their business cards. In these cases, take the time to explain any degrees and professional designations that you hold since these are highly prized by those who display their own credentials openly.

Most new immigrants, however, are not overly impressed with credentials, designations or degrees. Again, they are more likely to be concerned with the quality of the person with whom they are dealing. It works best for representatives to talk about themselves and their own families instead of real estate at the beginning of relationships with multicultural buyers or sellers.

To be successful with people from other cultures you must possess and display four personal characteristics: sincerity, honesty, integrity, and patience.

Sincerity means putting the customer's interests above your own. If you behave more like a consultant than just a salesperson, these customers will really appreciate it. Consultants do not need to make the sale, while a salesperson does. For instance, many blue-collar Puerto Rican Americans who are selling their homes in New York to buy a new home in Florida may not realize that there are few jobs for them in cities like Orlando or Tampa which offer mainly service jobs. A sincere salesperson would ask a customer to make sure they can obtain a job in the area before selling them a new home. The referrals generated by such an unusual act will more than make up for one customer who does not buy because he or she can't find a job.

Honesty means providing answers to questions if you know them and telling the customer when you don't know the answer. They don't want perfection and know you don't always have all the answers. However, home building and the issues that surround it are complicated, and they do want you to find the answers to their questions in a timely fashion. If you don't know the answer to a question, simply say, "You know, that's a great question. Let me find out the answer for you."

Integrity is saying what you are going to do and doing what you say. Consistency is a vital part of integrity. Be sure to write down any promises and keep them. So few salespeople do this, yet it is so very important to the customer.

Be clear on what you can and cannot do for new home buyers. Many think that because you work for the builder you can do anything, from turning a production job into a custom home for the same price to throwing in upgrades for free.

Patience means being prepared for endless questions and just answering them one at a time. Again, many of your buyers are first-time new home buyers who may not be comfortable with the language, culture, purchase agreements, home building or the home buying process. Your job is to educate them while keeping their discomfort with real estate and construction in mind.

"People from other cultures don't care how many units you've closed. They only care about one home – theirs."

Chapter 4

BUILDING RAPPORT WITH
PEOPLE FROM OTHER CULTURES

Culture can have a tremendous effect on the new home buying process. Everything from looking at models to negotiations with the builder to obtaining the loan and the closing are affected. Getting started properly and building a comfortable level of communication is crucial to success with people from other cultures.

Newly arrived in a strange land, multicultural customers try mightily to cope with customs they perceive as unusual. Recognize that they can be just as frustrated by American cultural peculiarities as people in this country are of theirs.

MEETING AND GREETING

Most of the world does not shake hands as we do in the United States. People in Asian cultures generally bow instead. Those from Latin America and Mexico may hug one another. Immigrant men from the Middle East kiss each other on both cheeks. Eastern Indians may put their hands together in front of the body and bow in the traditional "Namaste" greeting.

Multicultural Business Rule #1 is: Never assume! Many new home sales professionals have been embarrassed when they wrongly assumed that a customer is more comfortable with a traditional greeting. For instance, assuming that a Chinese customer will want to bow, they start right out in this manner. What happens is at the moment they bow, the customer, wanting to adhere to our customs, extends a hand. The embarrassed salesperson sees this out of the corner of his eye and quickly straightens up to offer a hand. The customer, seeing the other person begin his bow, quickly pulls back and starts to bow at the moment the representative proffers his hand. This dance could go on for quite some time, and the longer it continues the more tainted the relationship becomes.

To avoid this embarrassing scene, the salesperson should smile and hesitate for a moment before giving a greeting. This gives people walking into the sales office the opportunity to offer the kind of greeting that is most comfortable to them. Then, of course, the sales representative should make the same gesture, shaking hands, bowing or whatever is appropriate. It's simple, but you've got to be aware of how to handle this important part of the relationship.

Filipino customers are accustomed to shaking hands and expect a broad smile from an honest person. Offer coffee or tea to express your respect, and do what you can to make them comfortable. Most new home sales offices offer coffee, but not tea. Asians, in particular, do not like the taste of coffee.

After centuries under British rule, Eastern Indians seem to adapt quickly to Western habits. Shaking hands is normal behavior for both men and women. However, if the woman is older, a courteous and respectful nod of the head to acknowledge their presence might be better than a handshake, which could be interpreted as disrespectful. Traditional Indians may greet you with a "Namaste" which is a slight bow with the hands folded in prayer in front of the chest.

In Pakistan, a Muslim nation bordering on India, people greet each other with hugs, even in business settings. This is nothing like the Namaste greeting. In spite of the fact that these countries are neighbors, they have been at war for centuries. It's probably a good idea not to mention your Indian customers to Pakistanis and vice versa.

Arab men often greet each other with hugs and kisses on both cheeks. This greeting is quite a shock for Americans who find it unfamiliar, or fear that kissing or even hugging another man reflects negatively upon their masculinity. If you make the mistake of turning your face, you could really be embarrassed as one of those kisses lands on your lips! Muslim women, especially traditional ones with their heads covered, will usually avoid shaking hands with men.

Men in Eastern Europe, Portugal, Spain, Italy and the Middle East will often kiss their male friends on the cheek in greeting. In Mexico, Greece, and much of Eastern Europe, men greet one another with an embrace and a hearty pat on the back. In Mexico, this *abrazo* is a measure of the friendship; the longer the embrace, the deeper the camaraderie.

There are even differences between different types of handshakes. For instance, Germans will expect a very firm but brief handshake, while the French consider such a greeting rude. They prefer a very soft and quick handshake.

Speak slowly and clearly to people who appear to have difficulty with English. If your customers still do not understand you, try to find another way of explaining yourself. You can illustrate your point; draw pictures or diagrams as you speak. Many cultures, especially Asians, might appreciate this because they have a written language built on pictures. Above all, DO NOT SHOUT; customers who don't comprehend your words are not deaf, just unfamiliar with English. (By the way, what good does shouting do for a deaf person anyway?)

EXCHANGING BUSINESS CARDS

Business cards carry more significance in other parts of the world than in the United States. Don't be quite so casual when exchanging cards with people from other cultures.

Characteristic of the culture, the Japanese have a whole ceremony built around the initial greeting, including a prescribed exchange of business cards. Always be prepared to follow the customer's lead; if they bow with a business card extended, be prepared. Cards are generally proffered with both hands and a slight bow. Offer your card with the left hand as you accept theirs with your right. Which hand you use to accept the customer's card is crucial since the left hand is believed to be "unclean" in much of Asia and the Middle East. Receive the customer's card with your right hand, otherwise they might be highly offended.

You may wonder why there is such a belief about the left hand or why there seem to be no left-handed people in Asia and the Middle East. The reason the left hand is considered unclean is that in many other countries, the only thing people regularly use it for is bathroom duties. If a child shows a tendency to use the left hand for writing or eating, it is bound or tied behind his or her back until the use of the right hand becomes natural.

Do some people adhere to this belief strongly? One new home sales professional related an incident when he was doing some training for Arabs for the U.S. Army in the Middle East. At the end of the training session, a group of six American instructors were being honored by hundreds of local people with a feast in a tent in the middle of the desert. Part of the ceremony included a sumptuous meal and, of course, the U.S. servicemen were instructed to enter the line first. When the third American instructor, who happened to be left-handed, reached out for food with his left hand the entire proceeding instantly ceased as horrified guests quickly scattered in every direction into the desert. Needless to say, immediately following this embarrassing incident, the U.S. government provided cultural sensitivity training to all of its servicemen who would find themselves interfacing with local people.

Back to the card exchange ritual. Next, do something that most real estate professionals rarely do—make it a point to let the customer see you read their card. In fact, study it as if it were a holy book, since that level of significance attaches to business cards in Japan. Do your best to pronounce the name phonetically. Japanese names are usually polysyllabic (several syllables) and may be stressed differently, like Ta-KE-da or Ya-MA-shi-ta.

You should take the time to ask the customer to pronounce it for you, then write it down phonetically, but not on their card. You would no more write on a Japanese person's card than you would write on their face. This is the degree of importance they attach to their business cards.

If the customer is new to American business practice, explain what the terms "salesperson" or "sales representative" mean. Again, there are no counterparts in many other areas of the world. Ask about the Japanese person's business card and any title written on it, if appropriate. You may also wish to ask how long your potential customer has been with his or her company. Company loyalty is legendary in Japan, so don't be surprised if this is the only company the Japanese person has ever worked for. If you have been with your developer a while or the builder has a long history, you may wish to mention it at this time. These facts would carry a lot of credibility with Japanese nationals.

Bring out your business card from a nice, wooden, brass or leather card case on top of your desk. Don't pull it out of your shirt pocket because Japanese believe body heat dishonors your card. Respectfully place the customer's card into your desk or file. Never put a Japanese person's business card in a shirt pocket either for the reason mentioned above.

Men should never put the card in a wallet from your back pants pocket because such an act would represent intent to sit on the customer! Nor should a woman ever put the card in her purse and sling it below her waist -- again sitting on the customer. Do you now begin to grasp how important the business card is to a Japanese?

Never staple their card into your file. Would you put a staple in your customer's forehead? Instead, clip it into the file with a paper clip because you wouldn't want to lose it.

Once more for emphasis, never write on the business card. Also, never ever ask for another. To do so would mean you have lost the most important symbol of your customer's identity. For the same reason, never walk away from the table where you have placed the card because you might forget it. Doing so would be the same as forgetting the customer.

Sales representatives who work consistently with another culture may choose to help make the customers more comfortable by having their business information printed in the customers' language on the back of their business card. It's a good idea to avoid potential embarrassment by having someone who knows both real estate and the language translate the wording for your card.

Type size and all other aspects should be identical on both the English and Japanese sides. If your picture is on the English side, it must be on the other. Be sure any logo or other artwork appears on each side. Color printing on the English side means you use the same color on the foreign language side. Any difference, even calling the special side "the back," may be viewed as a slight to the customer, implying that the American culture and English language are superior to the Japanese. It might turn out to be worse than not taking the trouble to print the card in their language at all.

While giving out your home telephone number is generally not a good idea, people from India regularly do this. It is taken as a sign of accessibility and caring.

NAMES

People's surnames can give you a clue about where their ancestors came from. Asian names tend to give Americans the most problems and are the most difficult to pronounce. For instance, Chinese names tend to be monosyllabic, or one syllable. Common Chinese names include: Wong, Lee, Fong and Chin. On the other hand, Japanese surnames are usually polysyllabic such as Takeda, Watanabe and Yamashita. Prevalent Vietnamese names are Nguyen, Tran and Vu, whereas Korean's are Kim, Park and Shin. In Pakistan, the name "Khan," meaning "Lord," is prevalent because it used to indicate people from the upper classes, so now a large number of people from this country use this name.

The first thing to do with someone who has an unusual name is to have him or her write it out for you on a piece of paper. Most salespeople feel embarrassed when they can't pronounce a name, but more successful representatives make a point to get the pronunciation right. Ask the customer how to properly say his or her name and write it out phonetically such as Yamashita might be written out: Ya - mah – she – tah. The customer will really appreciate the salesperson's effort.

Next it is important to establish which is the surname. A name like "Lee Wong Kong" can easily confuse salespeople about which is the last name. Be aware that in many Asian cultures the family is so important, that by law the surname is written first, so be sure to ask. However, you must ask in the right way or you will increase the confusion. To ask, "Which is your last name" would probably elicit the response "Kong" in the previous example because it is written last but is not necessarily the surname. With Asians or any other group, try asking, "Which is your family name?" Most will understand that you want to get their surname right.

This technique is especially important when dealing with the Vietnamese, who often place their first names last. "Nguyen Van Dong" is using "Dong" as a first name and "Nguyen" as the surname. To use the name that comes last with the buyer would result in your calling your customer the equivalent of "Mr. Bill" for the entire transaction! Again, ask which is the family name.

Vietnamese women may have three or four names, all different from the husband. It is common in their country for a woman to retain her family name if there are no sons to carry on the name. The grandmother may have passed along another family name as well – hence the fourth name.

This is similar to the practice in the Latino or Hispanic culture, where people have two surnames – one from the father and a second from the mother's family. When she marries she will usually keep both surnames and add her husband's family name. In general, only one is used most of the time, but the full name is brought out in business and other formal settings.

Be sure to make copies of the correct spelling, phonetic pronunciation and family names of your customers, along with the gender designation. Then distribute to everyone in your company from design and decoration to finance, service and construction. It makes no sense to take such pains in getting the customer's name right, only to have someone else in the company undo it all by pronouncing it wrong or calling people by their first name, believing it is their surname.

Many support staff in new home companies have complained to the author that it's very embarrassing to try to call a customer for information and not know which person they are trying to reach or whether the phone number is for the husband or the wife. Be considerate and professional by making this information available to anyone you think might come in contact with your customers throughout the entire transaction.

When you introduce yourself to customers from other countries you must take your time with your own name. If it is difficult for others to pronounce (you should know this by now) try to find a way to make it easy to remember. Some American names are difficult for Asians to pronounce. The Japanese have a great deal of difficulty distinguishing between the English letters "L" and "R." For instance, top sales representative Ralph Roberts' name might be pronounced by some Japanese as "Lalf

Loberts." In this case he just might ask them to call him something else that they can pronounce.

We in America are relatively informal people and are quick to use each other's first names. It's usually best to be a bit more formal and not call a client by his or her first name unless invited to do so.

Use of first names in the Asian culture is rare. Calling an older Asian or Indian by his or her given name might be viewed as a high insult. It's usually best to call all of your customers "Mr.", "Mrs." or "Ms." unless and until they invite you to call them by their first name.

The Japanese are an extremely formal people who almost never call one another by the first name, even if they have been acquainted for years. They commonly call each other by the last name with the suffix "San," a non-gender specific title meaning "Mister," "Mrs." or "Miss." "Yamamoto-San," then, might refer to any person of that name.

The very formal Germans are also very slow to use the first name. To call an older person from this culture by his or her first name would be the height of disrespect.

LANGUAGE

Learning to deal with other languages can be one of the most frustrating parts of working with people from other cultures. On the other hand, once you dig beneath the surface it can also be a very enlightening and enjoyable experience.

For instance, some people wrongly assume that all of the Asian languages are the same, since they sound similar to the untrained ear. Many are surprised to learn that each culture has its own distinctive language and writing that usually cannot be understood by the other.

The Chinese language actually consists of many different dialects that are incomprehensible to each other. The language of most Chinese Americans whose ancestors came to America in the 1800's is Cantonese, of which there are several distinct dialects. The main language of China today is Mandarin, which many have learned to speak in addition to their own unique village language. If villagers cannot speak Mandarin they may not be able to communicate with people outside their village except through writing, which is universal.

Chinese writing is in "ideograms," which are characters that often look like a whole word or idea, as opposed to a single letter as in English. There are over 40,000 ideograms in the Chinese language.

Japanese speak a totally different language from the Chinese, while their writing is similar, having been developed from Chinese ideograms. Japanese writing is called "Kanji."

Likewise, Koreans speak a separate language from the Chinese and Japanese. They have their own alphabet called Han'gul which consists of 40 characters. Of all the Asians, Koreans are considered to be the most emotional group and can get quite demonstrative during conversation.

In India, 20 major languages and hundreds of dialects are spoken. Because of the Indians' history as a British colony until 1980, most are comfortable with speaking English.

India's Pakistani neighbors speak four major languages, every one different from the impressive array of tongues spoken in India. However, the national language of Pakistan is *Urdu.* It is also spoken in the heavily populated northwest part of India.

The Filipinos speak *Tagalog,* which has several different dialects. Their writing is again unique and distinct from other Asian groups.

In the Middle East, Muslims such as Arabs must learn Arabic in order to study the Koran. Arabic is the second most widely used form of writing after the Roman alphabet. Over 200 million people in the world speak Arabic. Arabic is a very expressive language, and those with untrained ears can easily mistake a spirited conversation for an argument.

Another misconception is that Hispanics all speak Spanish. Many Brazilians, for instance, speak and write Portuguese due to the influence of that culture on residents.

While a majority of people from Guatemala speak Spanish, about 53% come from Mayan Indian background. These people may speak any one of 20 native dialects.

ATTIRE

Dress well when meeting most people from other cultures. Latin Americans, Germans and Japanese, especially, look at how you dress to determine how successful you are.

African Americans may also judge you by how you dress. Best to dress formally at the beginning until you know how your clients feel about this issue.

Obviously, if you are working in a resort community more casual attire may be appropriate. Ask your sales manager or use your own judgment when it comes to a dress code at your community.

EYE CONTACT

Eye contact does not carry the same meaning among all cultures. In America, steady eye contact indicates honesty and a sincere interest in what the other party has to say. Western society expects the person with whom we are communicating to look us in the eye. It is so ingrained into our culture that we are suspicious of anyone who doesn't give us direct eye contact.

In some cultures, averting the eyes is a display of respect for the person who is speaking. It can be a bit unnerving, but the best course is to resist the temptation to try gaining eye contact. Depending on the culture involved, it could be considered rude and intrusive.

Vietnamese and Koreans may avert the eyes to demonstrate respect for authority. Japanese feel strongly that prolonged eye contact is threatening, rude and disrespectful. Asian Indians and the Pakistanis also eschew direct eye contact as respectful.

Quite opposite to these groups are the Middle Easterners. An Arab looks directly into the eyes of the person he intends to communicate with, for what Americans see as an uncomfortably long time. This practice stems from the belief that looking into the eyes helps one see the truthfulness and integrity of the other person. They believe that the eyes are quite literally the windows of the soul.

African Americans interpret good eye contact as a sign of sincerity and honesty. Like most Americans, they perceive that it implies honesty and integrity. But be aware that African Americans tend to use more eye contact than Caucasians when speaking and less when they listen.

Hispanic and Latino men like direct eye contact; this is known as *gada a gada* or "face-to-face." Nevertheless, it is considered impolite to look at women from the Hispanic culture with long-lasting eye contact. An intense gaze can be taken as a show of romantic interest. Instead, cast polite glances of short duration in the direction of a Latina woman, only enough to show you are paying attention.

Many Native American tribes dislike strong eye contact. Navajos teach their children that a stare is like an "evil eye."

Differences in attitude toward eye contact can result in unfortunate misunderstandings. In Los Angeles, Korean businesses in African American neighborhoods were targeted for complaints because many residents felt the shop owners showed disrespect toward them. One reason cited for this charge was the lack of eye contact they received from Korean proprietors. It was generally unknown in the community that Koreans avert their eyes as a sign of respect. But African Americans expect very direct eye contact for the same reason. Is it any wonder this cultural difference led to ill feelings?

BODY LANGUAGE

Posture is important in any number of cultures. Asians in general believe that control of the body shows control of the mind. Slouching or leaning is taken as a sign of lacking discipline.

The Japanese prefer to see a firm, upright posture with both feet firmly planted on the ground. They feel that such a posture exemplifies a solid person. Anything less implies that a person is not trustworthy.

Middle-Easterners find it offensive when someone crosses his legs with the bottoms of the feet pointed in their direction. To do so is one of the highest insults in that part of the world because they feel that the foot is the lowest part of the body and the sole of the shoe, the dirtiest. People from the Middle East cross their legs as an intentional, overt insult to the other party. Showing someone the bottom of your foot says you are looking for a fight. Many people from Thailand interpret this action in the same way.

In fact, body language itself is often different from what Americans expect. Expressive body language is carefully avoided in most Asian nations, for fear it may betray one's feelings. The Chinese, for example, do not readily display emotion because concealing it is deeply rooted in their culture. The "inscrutable oriental" myth is rooted in the perceived need for "face saving" or preserving honor. A display of emotions is seen as a breach of the face-saving custom because it disrupts harmony and may cause conflict.

At the other end of the body language scale, African Americans tend to be more emotional, intense, and enthusiastic in their demeanor and use of voice than white Americans. You can usually feel safe in being less restrained and more demonstrative in your dealings with people from this culture.

If you are left-handed, try to minimize the use of this hand especially when eating in front of or accepting a business card from people of other cultures. Again, a great number of people whose background lies outside the United States believe that the left hand is "unclean" and should only be used for hygiene purposes.

Keep your hand gestures small and close to your body

when speaking to Asians. The American habit of making large expressive gestures out to the sides of the body can be quite intimidating for this group.

Likewise, keep your facial expressions neutral as well with Asians. Again, the Chinese believe that displaying too much emotion disrupts harmony.

On the other hand groups like Italians, Middle Easterners and, as we have said, African Americans tend to be more expressive than Caucasian Americans do. Salespeople from this country might find conversations with these groups as intimidating as Asians find it speaking with them.

PERSONAL SPACE

New home salespeople in America should be aware that the "personal space" we are used to is not the same in all cultures. For business conversations in this country, we are used to shaking hands, dropping them and then talking. This usually leaves two or three feet of space between the parties, a distance that is comfortable for most Americans. Anything less implies a more intimate conversation and anything more implies mistrust or psychological distance between the parties.

Some Americans think people from the Middle East are "aggressive" because they will stand barely a foot away during conversation. Little do we know that they have a saying about holding a friendly discussion. The saying is, "I want to feel your breath on my face." Sales representatives should be aware of this difference and <u>not</u> back up should a Middle Easterner stand uncomfortably close. It might be especially difficult for an American female salesperson to maintain such close quarters talking to an Arabian male, for example. But lest you offend, stand your ground! Otherwise they may chase you all over the sales office or trailer to have a conversation.

On the other hand, the more formal Japanese might shake hands or bow at our customary three feet, then step back another foot. In that case, do not try to shorten the distance. You might end up chasing these people all over town violating their more distant personal space. This will not win high marks in the rapport-building Olympics.

In India there are very complex rules about how closely members of one caste may approach members of other classes. It is best to wait and see how much distance an Indian customer establishes during conversation.

In cultures seemingly similar to America's, like those of Scotland and Sweden, there is additional distance to personal space. In Germany, private space is practically sacred and never to be violated lest severe consequences ensue.

As always, do not assume. Wait to see what your customers do and take your cues from them to do likewise.

PHYSICAL CONTACT

Many cultures are not as "touchy-feely" as Americans are. A male sales representative should never touch a traditional Japanese woman, as this would be the near equivalent of rape. Similarly, a male sales representative should not put his hand on a Chinese woman's forearm or shoulders, however friendly the gesture might be meant. The German culture is very formal, and they consider any other greeting than their firm handshake highly offensive.

On the other hand, Puerto Ricans are very tactile people. A recent study observed people from this island country and other cultures in social settings. The Puerto Ricans touched each other an average of 180 times an hour, while people in Florida made physical contact two times an hour. In England there was no contact at all.

Studies show that African American males touch each other during conversation more often than European Americans. African American women tend to touch each other while talking about twice as often as Caucasian females.

GIFT GIVING

You may want to bring a small but thoughtful gift when presenting the keys to new homeowners. Although some Americans think that giving gifts in a business relationship is a form of bribery, other cultures use presents to continue a relationship after the home has been purchased. Therefore, you should be aware of which cultures regularly exchange gifts in a business setting and what is fitting. Business gift giving is common, or expected, in South Korea, India and Japan.

The Japanese are among the most enthusiastic gift givers in the business world. In fact, it's a $92 billion a year industry in that country.

Japanese celebrate most American holidays and have even invented a few of their own to increase the opportunity for gifting. They exchange presents as a matter of course in business meetings, especially at midyear (July 15th) and year's end (January 1st). It is also considered good manners to bring flowers, cake or candy when invited to a Japanese home.

One caveat about exchanging gifts with the Japanese is to never outspend your customers or you will cause them to lose face. Having lost face, they may never be comfortable in your presence again.

The problem is selecting a gift that is neither more expensive nor more generous than your customers' before you know what they are giving you. The author's solution is to ask permission to open their gift in their presence. While this is not commonly done in Japan, they realize it is an American custom and accept it. I then excuse myself saying that I have forgotten their gift in my car. When I know I am meeting Japanese customers, I keep three gifts of different values ($25, $50 and $100) in the trunk of my car at all times. Upon reaching the car I do my best to pick the most appropriate one. When in doubt, I always err toward a slightly less valuable present than they have given me. New home salespeople may wish to do something similar or keep the gifts in their desk in the sales office.

The surest way to choose an appropriate present for any customer is to probe gently and listen for their interests when you first speak during the home buying and building process. For those who show an avid interest in sports, a set of golf balls of a respected brand usually sets well. For people that drink alcohol, a bottle of fine liquor—many Japanese are partial to good Scotch—makes an excellent gift, while a high quality crystal piece is a most impressive offering.

Listen carefully to your customers. Some people, such as Muslims, are prohibited by their religion to drink alcohol. Giving an Asian a knife or a pair of scissors carries an inherent risk. In their cultures, anything that cuts symbolizes the severing of a relationship, the polar opposite of what you meant to create. It's wise to also avoid clocks as a gift for Asians, as they can symbolize death, or the "winding down" of life. Presents consisting of four of anything should be avoided since this is an unlucky number to many Asians. You may have noticed that Japanese and Chinese tea sets usually come with either five or six, never four cups.

Wrapping your gift is also an important consideration. The Japanese prefer rice paper and soft pastel colors to the bright hues most often displayed on Americans' gifts. Both Chinese, Japanese and Koreans dislike white wrapping paper intensely, since that is the color attached to death in both cultures.

Fortunately for the average sales representative's budget, most other Asian cultures are less disposed to gift giving than the Japanese. Indeed, many Europeans consider it an insult to give a gift before business is completed. Others take it as an open attempt at bribery. Check with sales representatives who have done business with customers from the culture you are concerned with before you choose a gift.

GETTING ACQUAINTED

After the greeting comes the critical stage of rapport building. This is where the salesperson and customer get acquainted and decide whether they wish to proceed with the relationship. This step is crucial for people from other cultures. These customers are more concerned with the quality of the builder and the person with whom they are planning to do business, than with degrees, awards or even experience the salesperson might possess.

As with any new potential customer, salespeople can talk

about any subject that seems natural—anything but real estate or construction. One new home salesperson couldn't understand why she couldn't get Japanese buyers to talk about the models in her subdivision. She would have had more success commenting on their children.

Take an interest in your customer; ask about family, work, and leisure time activities. Almost any subject is acceptable in search of common interests other than the usual American taboos – sex, politics and religion. The builder representative should not discuss business until the customer brings it up. It will rarely be introduced before the customer feels sufficient rapport has been established to make them comfortable with you.

People from other cultures take their time choosing a builder and a salesperson because they expect this to be a long-term relationship. In America we tend to have many informal personal relationships and only a few deep, lasting friendships. In other cultures, even business relationships seem to run more deeply.

Also remember not to lump the various cultural groups together. While Pakistan is the next door neighbor to India, it is probably not a good idea to talk about your Indian customers to Pakistanis. There has been a long history of animosity between the countries. Puerto Ricans from the island consider themselves a totally separate class from Puerto Ricans who have lived in New York for many years. Remember that China, Korea and Japan have all had their differences over the years, so keep them separate in your mind as in your conversations.

If you find yourself stuck for questions to ask, remember the old newspaper reporters' adage of the five "W's": Who,

What, When, Where, Why and How. For example, the "Who are you" line of questioning could include, "What country did you or your ancestors come from?" and "What size was your family?" "What" questions might be, "What languages do you speak" or "What schools did you attend?"

The "When" might lead you to ask, "When did you arrive in America?" or "What time do you usually take your evening meal?" Some good "Where" questions are, "Where are you living now" or "Where have you traveled to over the years?" A "Why" question could address issues such as "Why did you choose to live in this area?" or "Why have you come at this time?"

Finally, your "How" questions could include, "How did you travel to America," "How long do you plan to live here?" or "How many are there in your family?" If conversation hasn't become natural and free flowing by this time, you may never develop rapport with this customer. Frankly, you may want to consider referring them to another salesperson and expect a referral or two in exchange.

Filipinos do not generally like to be asked questions. They are proud that their country has one of the highest literacy rates in the world, at 85%. Consequently, asking too many questions could make them feel you think they are not very intelligent. Therefore, the sales representative should check their tolerance for questions by beginning with open-ended questions.

Hispanics have a strong sense of pride in their ethnic roots. With this in mind, find out their country of origin and learn as much as you can about it. See if you can't establish a mutual education agreement wherein you promise to teach them all they need to know about real estate. In turn, they exchange information about their language and culture.

Different and distinct groups live side-by-side in the Saudi Arabian peninsula. Three in number, they are: Nomadic and semi-nomadic pastoral peoples, farmers and urban dwellers. Each has its own characteristics and special interests. In real estate, you are most likely to find property buyers from among urban dwellers, since they are most likely to have the means to buy American real estate. Again, you will probably be expected to brag about your accomplishments with this group.

Saudis place great value on family, and most subscribe to the Islamic religion. Discussions about family or family history are always a good place to begin rapport building. It is vital in relationships with believers to know that Islam affects all facets of life and behavior for Saudis. Especially significant is that Islam teaches that only Allah, or God, decides the future.

Koreans use a special vocabulary for different degrees of social status, depth of intimacy and for formal and informal occasions. When meeting a Korean they expect to begin with small talk so that they can determine what kind of language to use with you.

Some cultural groups can be very open in conversation. Others may ask searching personal questions of the sales representative. It is common for family-oriented Chinese customers to ask salespeople about marriage and how many children they have. In fact, most current immigrants are quite family oriented. Questions on this subject usually elicit lengthy and intense responses. Some that are considered intrusive in our culture are expressions of good will in theirs.

Other cultures are less verbal. Asian cultures expect the listener to read between the lines. When conversation with a

Japanese lags, most Americans feel they must step in and get it going again. We feel constrained to fill a conversational void with almost anything, even pointless chit-chat. Doing that with a Japanese suggests that you are not a very deep thinker, or worse, that you hope to conceal something with your chatter.

Silence is important to communicating with Eastern Indians. Hindus believe that wisdom and peace come from communicating with yourself in meditation. Success with customers from these cultures requires you to learn to be comfortable with silence—a condition most of us Americans find unsettling at best.

Don't be surprised if a multicultural customer asks one of the most prohibited questions in American society, "How much money do you make?" They usually think you make more than you actually do, but most immigrants think all Americans are rich. What else would you think from people who watch "Lifestyles of the Rich and Famous" leading them to believe that everyone here has solid gold toilet seats and dog bowls?

However you decide to answer this question, the answer will almost always be less than they think. If you take the time to explain how little you really do make and how hard you work compared to most people's perception, there will be fewer demands for part of your commission. Even if you are one of the top salespeople in your company or service area, it is probably best not to mention this fact to people from other cultures. Not only is it not important to most cultures, it could be a perceived as a negative. Many groups value cooperation over competition, and pointing out your own accomplishments could be seen as evidence of a character flaw. The Japanese have a saying on this issue, "The nail that sticks up gets hammered down." Other cultures that are more cooperative than competitive are African Americans, Asian and Pacific Islanders and Hispanics.

New home salespeople will find that some multicultural peoples take longer than others do to develop rapport. With the Chinese and Japanese many meetings may be needed, during which you will be expected to talk about anything except real estate. They are ready to get down to business when they are certain you are a trustworthy and honest person.

For similar reasons, Jamaicans prefer that their relationship with a salesperson and builder develop slowly and without pressure. They want to see that you are more interested in their needs than in your commission. Jamaica is a tourist destination with a very relaxed pace; Jamaicans will likewise appreciate a slower pace. Also, because there is a shortage of homes available for purchase in their land, sales representatives usually meet customers at the property they want to see. Let this kind of customer know what services you offer and what you expect in return. Be sure to include punctuality on the list.

Jamaican men are "macho" and detached from everyday details, while the women are characteristically strong willed. Between the two, the woman usually makes the decision on a home. The bluntness of Jamaicans in normal conversation can startle Americans because their culture accepts them saying what's on their minds. Both men and women may lead you to think they're angry because their culture speaks with passion. On the contrary, people from that island are among the friendliest in the hemisphere.

Children are treasured by everyone, especially people from other cultures. If you show kindness and concern for the children of your customers, rapport will build more quickly.

However, you must be aware of a couple of issues. First, never touch the head or tousle the hair of children from Vietnam, Laos, or Cambodia. In these cultures it is believed that the head is sacred because it houses the spirit. It is said that if the young spirit is not strong enough to be touched the child could become ill. We in America believe that our souls live in the heart area. Who's to say which is more correct?

The same prohibition against touching the head holds true for African American children, but for different reasons. Slave owners used to rub the heads of slave children for good luck; this is still a sensitive issue to people from this culture today.

New salespeople will be pleased to learn that people from other cultures are most concerned about the quality of the person with whom they are contemplating doing business. They're not easily impressed by long years of experience or a long history in the business. Multicultural people recognize that while experience can be gained, being a trustworthy person cannot. If they find you to be a good, honest person they will probably be glad to work with you.

You can talk about almost anything with multicultural customers, but there are some sensitive subjects you are better off avoiding. The subject of the Peoples' Republic of China is a political hot potato with the Taiwanese. Koreans would rather not discuss the issue of North and South reunification, and the Chinese in general are very reserved on the subject of sex. African Americans prize their families, but single parenthood is a sensitive subject, since African American male slaves were often removed from their families and required to work apart. Initiate a conversation about children and you will rarely go wrong in any cultural environment. Kids represent a universally acceptable subject.

Arabs habitually boast among themselves about their own culture's superiority, but never discuss personal shortcomings. Anyone doing business with them is expected to display this social characteristic. But while they rarely talk about their own, they are far from shy about pointing out others' shortcomings, real or perceived. Pity the real estate sales representative who fails to serve them well. That unfortunate person will become the subject of after-dinner conversation for a long time to come!

As a natural part of the rapport building process, include education for your potential customers about the home buying and building business. It's not just what you do for a living and how much you earn that engages their interest, but how you explain the entire process itself. In addition, professional respect will grow with every opportunity to gently inject business talk into matters that don't directly relate to the business at hand.

MULTICULTURAL WOMEN

It's a fact that most of the rest of the world is not as sexually liberated as the United States. For instance, Saudi women are considered less capable than men are. Their life roles are strictly prescribed in the Holy Koran. They are expected to yield subserviently to men in all matters. In the universities, women are not permitted to attend the same classes as men. Traditional Saudi women are not allowed to drive or even ride a bicycle. It is indispensable to understand these facts in any relationship with Saudis.

You should not bring up the subject of his wife to a male customer from the Middle East unless he mentions it first. She may not accompany him to look at property nor will she sign papers. In their home country everything is owned by the man, so if you have legal requirements that the wife sign documents, you must be emphatic but firm. To gain cooperation you will probably have to explain several times that the American government requires it.

Both the Hispanic and Filipino cultures are very male-dominated and may not afford women the equity they are used to here. Some American saleswomen become irate when unequal treatment takes place in their sight. Whether you are male or female, it is wise to be aware that this can occur and decide in advance how you will respond. It's unlikely you are going to change thousands of years of culture and religious belief with a fifteen-minute lecture on sexual equality.

WOMEN SALESPEOPLE

Women new home salespeople need to be aware of several beliefs that can affect them. First of all, they should dress conservatively for working with customers from other cultures. Many do not view short skirts as fashionable. Asians are most comfortable if a woman's skirt at least covers the knees when standing.

Saudi Arabian men are more comfortable working with women sales representatives who cover their arms and legs. In some Middle Eastern countries, it is a crime punishable under Islamic law for a woman to show any skin in public. Bare shoulders could be quite distracting to Arab men who are not used to this sight outside the home.

Latin American men, especially Brazilians, may stare and

make comments about women. You need to be polite but firm when dealing with men from this country.

Working with Japanese customers, you should be aware that this culture has for centuries considered the nape of the neck an erogenous zone. You may want to cover your neck with a scarf or high collar to keep their minds on business!

Some American women stand up straight to project confidence and business ability. Unfortunately, Asians consider this too masculine a stance; a slightly hunched pose is preferred. It is especially important for taller women salespeople to adopt this position.

Perhaps unexpectedly, men from the Philippine culture may actually prefer female sales representatives, thinking them more trustworthy than men. Remember the issue of *la gai;* they do not associate it with women.

Likewise, Middle Eastern men may prefer working with female salespeople for the same reason. While you may not receive the same level of respect you are accustomed to, they will tend to trust you more than they would a man.

You may find men from other cultures trying to deal with men in your company instead of you. If this appears to be the case you may want to refer them to a male salesperson.

Women salespeople must learn to walk the fine line between being businesslike and feminine when working with people from other countries. Most multicultural men prefer women who are unassertive.

Finally, some cultures just don't approve of women working outside the home. More Latino men than European Americans feel that women should not hold jobs other than homemakers. Decide in advance how you will handle this issue.

DINING WITH MULTICULTURAL CUSTOMERS

You may have occasion to have lunch or dinner with new home customers during or after a transaction. Dining out is an area where cultural differences in manners and what is considered polite can confuse Americans. A Chinese offered more food over lunch or dinner will probably refuse two or three times before accepting reluctantly. Be prepared to ask at least three times or your guest might go hungry! The Taiwanese who learns that you haven't had lunch feels obliged to drop everything and take you out to eat.

Any time you take prospective customers out to eat to help build rapport, be sure you know what kinds of food they like as well as what they might find repellent. The Chinese do not eat raw meat, so the very idea of taking them out for "steak tartare" (raw beef) would probably make them nauseous.

Hindus do not eat beef as it violates the religious belief that cattle house the souls of the departed. As a matter of faith, Muslims do not eat pork. Their religion is sometimes confused with the Hindu religion of India, but is separate and dissimilar.

You also need to be aware of eating practices in the country from which your customers hail. Chinese and Japanese eat with chopsticks. Traditional Arabs eat with the fingers of the right hand, while scrupulously holding the left, the unclean hand, in the lap.

Even today, Middle Eastern women usually eat separately from the men. Also, traditional Middle Easterners eat with their hands.

The Chinese will engage in boisterous discussions over a meal, while many Japanese prefer long periods of silence. If the conversation lulls during a meal with a Japanese, remember to fight the temptation to fill the void with idle chit-chat as we do in America.

FINANCES

You will probably want to get the customers pre-approved for a loan as early in the new home buying process as possible. Use care and sensitivity in approaching the subject of obtaining a loan with people from outside the United States.

Almost all new immigrants are at least somewhat private about their financial affairs. Think about it, had you recently arrived in a strange country would you go around publicizing your assets and debts? Hardly.

The subject of borrowing must be explained as a normal business practice in this country. Few new immigrants are familiar with American lending practices. In fact, many Asian cultures consider it shameful to owe money to anyone. Explain that here it is customary for a bank to lend money to a borrower who pays the money back with interest to compensate the bank for the use of its cash. In this country it is a standard business arrangement.

The next delicate area of discussion is how much the customer has for a down payment. Asians, in particular, are reluctant to give this information to anyone. In fact, just asking about this initial deposit could literally endanger the customer's life. Sound odd? Well, many people from this culture do not believe in putting their money in banks due to their instability in the home country. Therefore, they may keep huge sums of cash savings in the family home. This explains why there are so many home robberies of Asians. It isn't that they have more expensive stereos and TVs than everyone else, which is what you may have thought prior to reading this book.

It is an unwritten rule in law enforcement that the amount of cash taken in a home robbery is rarely disclosed. If the general public knew the amounts of money some groups keep outside of banks, there might be a spate of home invasions committed by people outside of this community.

A distrust of banks is also common in the Hispanic community. The author personally knows of one Hispanic investor who lost over $75,000 in cash at gunpoint from robbers who invaded his home.

Recognize that many Hispanics will deal strictly in cash, at least for a down payment. They may not have any money in the bank and virtually no credit cards. People who know Mexico understand why Hispanics don't trust their money to banks. In the past, their savings devalued substantially just sitting around at little or no interest. Yet worse, the rampant corruption they have seen as common banking practice could cause the loss of their entire life savings.

In order to obtain a loan for Hispanics without verifiable credit history you must seek out a loan officer who understands the issue. Those who are willing to use "alternative credit checking measures" will look to verify that the customer makes gas, electricity or other payments such as those for telephone, cable television or medical bills promptly.

So how can you know which model or neighborhood to show Asian or Hispanic buyers if you can't ask about the down payment? The simplest way is the "menu" method. Show them the amount of cash required and the monthly payments for a 10% initial deposit with the bank financing 90%, twenty percent down with the bank financing 80%, and so on. Of course, remind them that they can pay all cash, as many do.

Don't forget to add Private Mortgage Insurance (PMI) to any loan under 23% down that requires it. If you neglect this additional monthly payment your customers will assume you lied to them and expect you to pay it.

In Bob Schultz's book, *Smart Selling*[SM] *Techniques*, he provides the following strategy that may be helpful when trying to determine the financial situation of your customers.

SITUATION

You want to discover customer's financial possibilities.

STRATEGY

To ask.

SST-SMART SELLING[SM] TECHNIQUE

> *"Our homes range from (state lowest amount) to (state highest amount), depending on the size of the home you select, the location and the amount of customization (or personalization) you choose to do." What would you like to see today?"*

The fact is that Asians are good savers who may not believe in banks. It's possible that they sold their property in the home country before coming here and have a large amount of cash on hand. Therefore, the option that will probably be most comfortable for these customers is the one that calls for them telling you the amount of money they have as a down payment.

Buying a home is not an emotional purchase for most Asians. They do not generally "fall in love" with a property;

rather, they consider it an investment. They will usually have done their homework and will already know how much they have for an initial deposit and what the payments will be. Thus, when they choose an option from your financing menu they usually have the initial deposit and monthly income to support the option they have selected. As long as they believe it is a good investment they are likely to buy it.

Building trust is the crucial step. Establishing your honesty is critical to the new home sales professional working with customers from other cultures. Telling them how much you earn is seen as an act of honesty because they know they will have to provide personal financial information to you. In other words, if you can't trust them with your income amount, how can they trust you with their private data?

Be cautious when discussing money with customers from other cultures. Some Asians, for instance, believe that to owe another person money is a shame and that all purchases, including homes, should be paid for by cash. Thus, the first discussion of money always marks a delicate moment.

Despite its prevalence here, buying on credit is not a generally accepted practice worldwide. In Korea, major credit card companies have offered the MasterCard and Visa for a relatively short time. As a result, many Koreans do not understand that a payment due on a certain date isn't just as acceptable a week or a month later. Because the principles of credit are poorly understood there, some buyers from this culture may have a history of late payments. This does not necessarily mean that they are poor credit risks, but you must find someone from a financial institution who knows this and is willing to handle the loan in spite of this cultural propensity. Otherwise, you may have to discuss the possibility of increasing the initial deposit in order to obtain a "quick qualifier" loan, the requirements for which are not as strict as those with lower down payments.

On the other hand, credit is rather easy to obtain with very little paperwork in places like Jamaica. For these customers, you must explain the importance of proper credit procedures, loan applications, verification of credit, employment, deposit funds, etc. Frankness in such matters is by far the best way to deal with Jamaicans. Since the realities of American lending practices are not within their experience, they need to understand that these things are required to obtain a real estate loan. Help them understand that these procedures are not optional, and shopping around for another lender will only waste time.

Finally, remind them that these are not your own, but every bank's requirements, and that failure to comply with all the qualifying factors and answer all the questions will only succeed in getting the application rejected. Expect to use all your professional knowledge, making sure all the "i's" are dotted and the "t's" crossed.

Many of your multicultural customers will be first-time home buyers unfamiliar with American customs and legal system. True, the grounds and rules may be unfamiliar, but be assured that they will learn at lightning speed. They got here after all, and are sharp enough to afford property. You will find that a lifelong customer may emerge from slowly and carefully going through the process and the required paperwork.

Chances are good that few multicultural customers have friends or relatives who have bought homes from whom they can learn what is involved. Indeed, with the strong drive to own property that many new arrivals have, they may be better able to find help among fellow immigrants than our own minorities do within their groups.

A 1998 study released by the Federal National Mortgage Association (FNMA) showed that while nearly 70% of white households in the United States reside in their own homes, only about 45% of African American families and 44% of Hispanics are homeowners. After decades during which real estate ownership was illegal, even the Peoples' Republic of China began allowing its citizens to own real estate in 1998.

While some do have a greater desire to own homes than their dominant culture, around half of all African Americans and a third of Hispanics expect special obstacles to home ownership, as contrasted with Caucasians. Many seem discouraged about home ownership, because they expect discrimination in housing and lending to hinder their efforts. Old beliefs die hard, even in the face of multiple state and federal laws making discrimination a very risky practice.

In fact, survey after survey shows that this impression is not mere paranoia, that some mortgage loan officers still require more documentation and paperwork from African American and Hispanic loan applicants than from Caucasians. For this reason, many who believe they have suffered from these kinds of discrimination are turning to the Internet for loans. They find that they can apply, verify all needed information and receive approval for a loan online without face-to-face contact at the bank. They believe there is less likelihood of prejudice being a factor in the process.

Inexperience with the process is another roadblock to home ownership for African Americans and Hispanics. The same FNMA study showed that around one-third of both of these groups did not believe that a history of paying bills late would impact their ability to obtain a home loan. Yet, as most experienced home buyers know, a credit history showing such things as timely car and credit card payments are crucial to getting a mortgage.

Many new home buyers do not realize there are many different financing programs available. Some believe they must have a 20% initial deposit and perfect credit to qualify for a loan. There may even be special first-time home buyer programs in your area from which they could benefit. Obviously, new home salespeople should make themselves aware of any special financing available in their areas or through their builder.

Be considerate of all your multicultural customers. If possible, provide information and loan applications in their own language. Many lenders, as well as builders and title companies, keep such translations on hand.

As you work with people from other cultures, make an effort to educate them about the requirements that home buyers must satisfy. Explain at the outset the importance of having at least one year of on-time payments for all bills before applying for a mortgage. Detail the other information that the lender expects, such as employment and initial deposit verification, copies of past tax returns and all else that applies.

Unless they know well in advance that they will have to satisfy such requirements, the customers may consider them unwarranted intrusions into their lives, or worse, that you created them. Explain early and make it clear that all such information is required from every borrower. If they don't know this, it is quite possible that they will indignantly seek out a sales representative who they think won't make them jump through these hoops.

SETTING LIMITS

Hard working Filipinos and other groups may expect their salesperson to exhibit those same hard-working qualities. If you give them your home phone number they may call you at home in the evening or on the weekends and expect you not only to be awake, but working diligently on their behalf. Many other new immigrants are the same way. You may wish to set some boundaries in this area by telling them that after 8:00 PM or before 8:00AM is "family time" around your home. Putting off-hours in these terms will usually be understood and respected by people from all cultures.

Many new home salespeople have commented that some Vietnamese parents tend to be a bit slower in monitoring and redirecting behaviors of their children which are usually considered unacceptable in the American culture. Examples of such are running through models and jumping up and down on couches or beds. This is possibly due to the fact that they have been through some of the most horrible conditions imaginable and therefore pamper their children so they won't remember or think of the difficult times. There is nothing wrong, however, about setting limits in your models as long as it is equally applied to all prospective buyers.

DECISION-MAKING

Treat the family members of your multicultural customers with respect. Your buyer or seller may seek their approval before committing to a certain neighborhood and model. Relatives may also be providing part or all of the initial deposit for a property purchase. In addition to that kind of help, family members often have further vested interests in the transaction.

While seniors in America are often the butt of jokes and viewed by some as useless, other cultures revere their elders because of the wisdom and knowledge they are believed to have accumulated over the years. At the other end of life, children are prized in a majority of cultures. Compliments and thoughtfully chosen presents can bring you big rewards.

Family and elders will often be included in the final decision to invest in a new home, even after a purchase agreement has been ratified. Therefore, be sure to seek their input before having a purchase agreement signed if it appears they exert significant influence.

Older relatives may also accompany your home purchaser on the final inspection of the new home before close of escrow. Assure yourself that everything in the home from the light bulb in the refrigerator to the float in the toilet is in perfect working order so that no relative of the customer makes a negative comment that kills your transaction.

Be aware that some Middle Eastern men may make all of the decisions about buying a new home for the couple. If the wife does not indicate a preference do not ask, since it could be a high insult to take away the husband's authority.

"Differences can impact the new home demonstration process -- be aware of and plan for them."

Chapter 5

DEMONSTRATING NEW HOMES TO
PEOPLE FROM OTHER CULTURES

Once you have prepared your buyers and built rapport, it's time to take them out to look at the models for the first time. During the presentation be sure to ask questions in order to meet your customer's needs. According to Bob Schultz, "A great salesperson asks a number of questions in the sales presentation, constantly probing for information and feedback."

Most people visiting a new home community have no idea how to look at models. This is evidenced by the fact that they will stand and wait for a salesperson to finish talking to a previous customer before looking at the models. Some may not know that there are models to view beyond your office. Others may not have a clue how to select the most appropriate model.

Some new home builders have developed pamphlets on how to view a new home project and some of the special amenities that buyers should look for. This is almost like a "self-guided tour" of a museum. It's especially helpful when foot traffic becomes heavy, and there isn't time to explain everything to the potential buyers who arrive at the same time in the sales office.

DIFFERENCES IN TIME

We Americans are fond of saying, "Time is money." We place great value on promptness and like to get down to business without delay. However, a short delay of five minutes here or in England isn't considered unusual or disrespectful. Germans, however, are sticklers for promptness; in their country, one minute's tardiness is considered quite rude. On the other hand, a delay of 15 to 30 minutes is quite acceptable in the Middle East. Japanese may be consistently 30 minutes belated, but will expect you to be prompt without exception. In contrast, Latin Americans expect you to arrive late. They take it as a sign of respect.

Latinos believe in *mañana,* meaning literally, "tomorrow." This does not imply laziness, but rather, a concept that the future is not definite. Therefore, they feel one should take the time to enjoy the here and now.

Even the walking pace is significant within many cultures. People from England and America tend to walk much faster than do those from Taiwan, Indonesia or Mexico. Be aware of the customers' conduct in this respect while you are leading them through models or around home sites.

In Italy it is perfectly acceptable to be two hours late, while an Ethiopian may be even later. It's not unusual for someone from the island of Java not to show up at all.

This sometimes frustrating cultural characteristic makes it important for new home salespeople to set the parameters in the rapport building stage of a relationship. We need only to explain how important it is to be on time. Salespeople need to tell customers that because their days are busy, with one task or appointment scheduled after the other, others may not be willing to work with someone who isn't available as expected. With some, you might even make light of this "American bad habit of rushing around 24 hours a day." But make it clear that it's vital to conform to it.

One of the best ways to present the concept of timeliness

to people from other cultures is to explain that if your other customers have to wait, it will make you lose face. If you work for a production builder, explain the importance of sticking to the production calendar. If you are employed by a custom builder, tell them why any delay caused by the buyer will add to their cost.

People from the Caribbean resort island of Jamaica are probably the most different from Americans in their attitude toward time. Their relaxed attitude often results in showing up two or more hours late for an appointment. Salespeople must educate them from the start about the critical importance of being punctual for appointments and at close of escrow. The best idea is to pick them up at home or office on the way to an important meeting. But if you do, don't expect them to be ready when you arrive. People from the nearby Caribbean island of Haiti have a similar perception of time to Jamaicans. They have the same relaxed attitude and will be as much as two or more hours late for appointments.

The Jamaican home buying market is so competitive because of the scant number of properties available, that sales representatives there just leave if a buyer does not arrive on time. In fact, it is usually such a "sellers' market" that resale agents who represent buyers do not drive customers to properties but rather expect to have the anxious buyers meet them at the home.

Japanese buyers will often arrive a half-hour late, but nonetheless expect the salesperson to be waiting for them with nothing to do. Fortunately, it is not too difficult to satisfy this mindset and avoid wasting your time. The author always assumes that Japanese customers will be punctual and arrives on time for the first meeting. If they get there 30 minutes after I do, the next time I will be ten minutes late, which will still make me 20 minutes early. This goes on until I have learned exactly what their customary appointment timing is and plan around it.

Like the Japanese, Filipino customers regularly arrive late by a half-hour to an hour. Like the others, they expect the salesperson to be waiting for them. Making you wait reflects positively on their importance in the context of the business being done, which is considered significant in that culture. In ours, it might be called "pecking order."

Customers from other countries, except Germany, England, and a few small nations, often take a more relaxed attitude towards time than most Americans are used to. You must educate all of your customers from the start about the value of your time and the fact that other customers are on time for most meetings. Otherwise, they may be perpetually late, yet expect you to spend the entire day with them.

THE IMPORTANCE OF NEW HOMES
TO SOME CULTURES

For most Americans, owning a new home means there will be no need for maintenance for the next five to seven years. However, the price to be paid for a new home is likely to be 10 to 15% higher than a pre-owned home, due to the "new home premium." In addition, new home sites may be smaller due to limited available land, making them somewhat less attractive than resale to some buyers. To choose between a new home and a resale home can be a tough choice. A new home is not such a big deal to most Americans.

Some resale agents try to dissuade their buyers from

looking at new homes because the commission paid to them, if any, may be less than to what they are accustomed. New home salespeople must realize this fact and be ready to counter the tactic some resale agents have of avoiding showing new homes.

Asians, in particular, prefer new homes to resale homes because there can be no "bad energy" in the home. Asians believe that what happens to the previous owner of a home can be transferred to them including murder, suicide and divorce. Resale agents usually know very little about the entire history of a home, especially if it is quite old. Do they really know if there has ever been an untimely death in the home? Probably not.

When confronted with the comment, "I can buy a comparable resale property at a lower price," a new home representative can simply respond, "That's possibly true, but you don't know if any bad energy has previously been created in that home. In this new home, you create your own energy."

It goes without saying that you must treat each customer individually regardless of cultural background, but there are some general tendencies you can expect. For example, many Japanese prefer newer homes. In fact, homes in Japan are often torn down when they have stood for only 30 or 35 years.

Asians tend to like bright, spacious kitchens for cooking and formal dining rooms for family dinners -- not always available in resale homes. They don't particularly care for dim, candlelit dinners so the availability of light dimmers is not a big plus.

The Chinese generally want natural gas stoves because they are more compatible with wok-style cooking than electric stoves. Some Hispanics like stucco exteriors and tile roofs, reminiscent of architecture in their home countries.

The Filipinos like homes that look expensive and opulent, like a palace. Friends and family members enjoy trying to outdo each other. For example, if Filipino customers hear that a friend paid $200,000 for a home, they may insist on buying one that costs $220,000.

They also seem to have an affinity for high ceilings, formal dining rooms and family rooms for entertaining. They would like three or more bedrooms and two full baths or more so that guests can be proudly invited to stay. Some in this cultural group look forward to guests, with an eye toward showing them how successful they have become. Many would be interested in an "in-law apartment" or "au pair" option to house in-laws or other family members who come to visit.

Outside the home, successful Filipinos prefer large lawn areas for entertaining, gardens for growing vegetables and flowers, and possibly a fish pond for good luck. Multi-car garages are often a high priority, since they and their driving-age children are all likely to have expensive cars to be sheltered out of the weather and sun. Two or more garages imply that they have achieved a certain level of status as well.

Many African Americans like formal dining rooms for traditional festive Sunday family dinners. Like many other Americans, they appreciate large yards for entertaining on holidays and weekends. The living room is also an important area for having guests.

Jamaicans look for homes with a certain sense of class and appeal. Obviously, the definition of such characteristics is entirely set by each customer's personal taste, but the home must look good from the outside and indicate high status. These customers care greatly what friends and family think of their homes. Listen carefully for what they do and don't find pleasing as you take Jamaican prospects through various models.

Affluent Jamaicans have worked hard for their success. Most of their island's population lives in grinding poverty. Those who have done well strive for perfection and want their homes to reflect their success. If the new home they select is fairly plain looking these customers will turn it into a palace with painting, furnishings, and decoration.

A word of explanation: From shortly after discovery by Christopher Columbus to 1961, Jamaica was under the rule of The British Empire and still strongly reflects British manners and mores. The island's inhabitants have a typically British sense of dignity and propriety. Thus, the impression a home makes from the outside is very important.

Jamaicans enjoy homes with large and expansive rooms. They like to surround themselves with grounds having enough room to enjoy plantings of lush flowers and vegetables. Their yards are sometimes showcases of tropical beauty. You can often guess that a homeowner comes from the Caribbean by the banana or papaya tree in the front yard.

Homes in Jamaica are very expensive, so properties in the United States appear to be bargain priced in comparison. A home that sells for $150,000 in California might cost two or three million dollars in the islands.

Haitians are not native English speakers and tend not to associate much with African Americans. Haitians tend to be more close-knit and clannish than Jamaicans, and you often find them looking for homes in neighborhoods with a substantial number of Haitians. They seem to prefer one-story homes with many rooms to house their entire family, as well as extended family members. Many like darker woods for trim and paneling.

There are two distinct groups of Puerto Ricans in America. The first are the Puerto Rican-Americans who moved to New York in the 1950s to work in the factories. These are English-speaking, blue-collar workers who are now moving to Orlando, Florida, and other locations to get away from big-city ills such as crowded schools and gangs. They are often selling their homes and moving with cash. The problem is that there are not very many blue-collar jobs in tourist locations like Orlando, so after a few years many have had to sell their Florida homes at a loss and move back to New York. It might be wise to council your Puerto Rican American customers about the job prospects before they acquire a home.

The other group of Puerto Ricans are those from the Island who consider themselves a separate class from the earlier immigrants. It's probably best not to mention your Puerto Rican American customers to those from the Island. The new immigrants are often buying second or vacation homes in the United States and have very different housing needs than the Americans of Puerto Rican descent.

Brazilians often prefer homes in a gated community for safety. Security is one of the major concerns in their home country and may demand homes in gated communities or those with garages that have direct access to the house itself for the same reason. They also seem to prefer lots of windows and high ceilings, while the land surrounding the home is not as important.

Venezuelans have similar housing needs as Brazilians. They particularly want as many bedrooms and full bathrooms as they can afford, so that friends and extended family can stay. The author has a Venezuelan friend who grew up in a home in that country that had <u>seven</u> bathrooms.

If your community has the option to turn a library or study into a smaller room with a bath, you should let your Hispanic customers know. They would much prefer this setup to a place where guests could read a few dusty books.

Argentines also have similar housing needs as Brazilians. They really like designer touches and to be able to customize a home.

Many Latins are not used to carpeting in their country due to the humidity and therefore prefer tile floors. Tile roofs and Spanish style homes are more common in their country as well. They invest in homes to live in forever, to pass down through the generations. Therefore, they may be interested in future expansion potential by adding on or adding a story.

On the other hand, homes in India are quite inexpensive compared to the United States. For instance, a Mediterranean-style home that costs $50,000 there could cost $400,000 here, depending on location. This difference is due to the fact that labor in India is much less expensive than here.

Pakistanis also favor big homes of 3,000 to 3,500 square feet and more, which sell here in some areas around $400,000. There are real estate agents in that country who provide services similar to those in this country, but for clarity, as an American new home salesperson you still ought to explain what you do for a living and how you get paid.

Colombians tend to look for modern style homes that are relatively affordable in their country. A three-bedroom, two-bath home costs about $50,000, while a classic Spanish style home could cost anywhere between one to two million dollars. In Colombia, owners are used to paying agents a 10% commission for bringing in the buyer, but listing agents are rare.

Many new immigrants look for homes similar to the ones in their home country. In Panama, the homes average around $50,000 for a three-bedroom, two-bath home. Most homes are one story, since it is a very hot and humid country. Many look for these types of homes in the United States although they are probably more expensive here, depending on location.

In Costa Rica, homes also average $50,000 but can be as high as $400,000 or more on the beach. Some homes there are elevated to keep snakes out of the home.

New home buyers from Europe look for properties that are sturdily built. Remember that homes that are hundreds of years old are common there. They may be a bit suspicious of American construction techniques which can appear to be "quick and dirty" to this group. Take a bit more time to explain how the builder makes the home last.

Middle Easterners seem to prefer single-story homes. They may be concerned that the toilets not point toward the east; devout Muslims may feel that it is disrespectful to face Mecca when going to the bathroom.

Schools with good records and high reputations are generally appealing to people from other cultures. Regardless of what we in this country may hear about the declining level of American education, those from outside this country usually view it as the vehicle for their children to get ahead in this society. Therefore, if the schools in the area have a good reputation, point out this fact. If possible, have supporting test scores from the schools for the customers to review.

Some cultures prefer homes within walking distance to good schools. Close proximity saves on commuting expenses, but that may not be the only factor to consider. In some cultures, like the Japanese, traditional women do not drive. Nearness to the schools makes it easy for parents or servants to escort the children to and from.

DEMONSTRATING NEW HOMES

It cannot be stressed too much that you are likely to be showing new home models to first-time buyers who are unfamiliar with American home buying customs. You must move slowly and explain every aspect of home buying and construction in detail.

It's not uncommon for multicultural customers to bring extended family members to look at new homes. Many people from other cultures respect the opinion of their peers. Some may be providing some of the financial support for the home.

If your community is near a cemetery it may negatively impact some buyers. In particular, many Asians do not want a home in such a location. More on this later.

It is essential to treat the Hispanic woman of the home with respect. Chivalry is not dead in this culture; it is usually appropriate to open doors for a Hispanic woman (unless the husband does so), solicit her opinion, and be attentive to her comments throughout the showing. The female spouse is the one most able to kill the sale if she doesn't like something. And since the home buying discussion will take place between the two spouses in their present home, you won't be there to offer counter arguments.

Many women from other cultures have difficulty believing that elegantly dressed and refined new home salespeople ever have to deal with the same mundane duties that they do. Whenever you are demonstrating the amenities of a model, say things like, "When I cook" or "When I do the dishes" or "When I clean." This will help them to better relate to you and believe the benefits of the appliances you are trying to demonstrate.

Most people from other cultures will not make the decision to buy a new home while looking at the models. They generally resist high-pressure tactics and will quickly leave if a new home salesperson employs such an approach. They usually go home and talk things over in detail before making a final decision. A home purchase is a big investment, and they are unfamiliar with property values, the American legal system and almost everything else about American real estate. The efforts you make to provide good and reliable information early in the relationship can bear fruit at this stage.

DIFFERENCES IN MEASUREMENT

It is surprising to Americans that most people around the world do not measure homes or land in square feet or acres the way we do here. The majority of countries use square meters for interior measurements and hectares or "apples" for outside dimensions. One hectare is 2.2 acres and an apple is 1.8 acres.

Koreans call their units of interior measurement *pyungs,* which equal one square meter. Japanese measure the inside of their homes using units called the *tatami,* which is the size of the traditional sleeping mat or approximately three feet by six feet or 18 square feet. Thus, an eighteen hundred square foot home would be 100 *tatami,* which is quite large compared to Japanese standards, where 50 *tatami* homes and apartments are standard. The land in Japan is measured by placing two tatami mats together to equal an area that is six feet by six feet or 36 square feet called a *tsubo*. Land that is, say 36,000 square feet, would be 1,000 *tsubo;* this would seem huge to a Japanese who comes from a country where it is impossibly unaffordable for the average person to own land.

It would be a very thoughtful and considerate gesture to help convert measurements into whatever units your customers are most comfortable with. It is also very easy to do, so ask if they would prefer to know home size in square feet or in some other unit.

"tatami"	*"tsubo"*
3' X 6'	*6' X 6'*
18sf	*36 sf*
Interior Measure	*Exterior Measure*
	1 Acre = 1210 tsubo

BUYING SIGNS

Most new home real estate salespeople rely on reading the "body language" of their customers to know whether they like or dislike a model home or community. Although this technique is effective with many multicultural buyers, some groups who exhibit less obvious physical buying signs, for example, Asians, can present a peculiar problem. They often express no body language at all. Remember that many Asians believe that "control over the body is control over the mind," so even if they like a home there is no outward evidence of their feelings. Also, remember that buying a home in America is not an emotional purchase for them, but an investment.

The only buying sign likely to come from Asian customers whose body language is non-existent is the very thing real estate professionals fear most: the whole group moves *en masse* to a corner and converses spiritedly in their own language. Most of us secretly fear that when others speak in a foreign tongue in our presence they are talking about us. But new home salespeople should learn to welcome these interludes because they are likely to be one of the only buying signs they will see.

Think about it: Do prospective new home buyers talk about a home they are not going to buy? No, they simply reject the property and go on to the next one. So when they go off and speak in another language, encourage them. Quietly exit from the room and let them talk--the longer, the better. Let them know that you will be available in the office or trailer when they are done.

Probably the only other obvious buying sign you will receive from multicultural new home buyers is the very uncomfortable question, "Are there other people like us living in this neighborhood?" It is a natural concern of people who know they look physically different from the dominant culture in America; they don't want to be the only one of their group in an area. However, new home sales professionals are prohibited by federal fair housing laws from discussing anything regarding the ethnic, racial, religious, age, familial status or disabilities of any of the homeowners in an area.

Potential new home buyers are perfectly welcome to obtain the racial statistics available from any Chamber of Commerce or other source, but you should not assist them in this endeavor. Some people are so concerned about this issue that they will sit in their cars for hours watching homeowners enter and leave a community. Again, this is a definite buying sign that should not be ignored by new home salespeople.

WOMEN NEW HOME BUYERS

Few cultures have progressed to the point the United States has in regards to equality for women. In many cases, the man does all the talking for a married couple. Some Asian and Middle Eastern males simply expect the woman to like whatever the man selects. This may irritate American women new home sales professionals; in such circumstances it's probably best to refer these customers to another salesperson. You will not dispel thousands of years of cultural imprinting with a lecture on women's rights and will surely lose the customer in the attempt. Filipino men make the ultimate decision to buy a home, while the wife will have decided on its style and location.

Brazil was once a very male-dominated society, but its women have made great strides towards equality in recent years. Now, Brazilian women usually make the decision on which home the family will buy. The husband then negotiates the actual details.

Listening carefully is the key to finding the right model and site for any customer. Pay attention to every comment made during the showing process. Once again, no customer is going to spend much time talking about a model that is not under serious consideration.

Be warned that people from cultures outside the United States are often quite adept at negotiating strategies and closing techniques. To say to a Hispanic customer, "Do you want to write a purchase agreement now or tonight?" would be instantly recognized as the classic "alternative of choice" close and could be taken as a demonstration of lacking respect. Use a natural close as the opportunity arises. Asking if they want upgrades is a great trial close. If they start naming upgrades, they have bought the model.

STEERING

It is especially important not to assume that people from any particular culture want to live in areas of the community occupied by people from the same culture. While most people of color do not want to be the only member of their group to live in an area, they do want to be free to choose where they live.

Apart from all else, assuming that a family of a particular ethnic background wants to live in a part of your community where others of their same ethnicity live constitutes illegally "steering" the customer. What if a valued customer asks you whether or not there are others of his or her same ethnic background living in your new home community? The following SST-Smart Selling[SM] Technique from Bob Schultz's book, *Smart Selling Techniques*, is one possible response that should enable you to diplomatically and *legally* handle this situation.

SITUATION

Customer asks, "What kind of people live here?"

(-or-)

"What's the ethnic make-up of the neighborhood?"

STRATEGY

First, to make absolutely sure that you don't violate Federal Law, while at the same time being tactful with your answer and maintaining a positive attitude.

SST-SMART SELLING[SM] TECHNIQUE

> The most tactful answer to the first question is:
> *"Very nice (or happy) people."*

If that does not satisfy them and they persist . . .

> Ask:
> *"Oh, I'm just curious, why do you ask?"*
> Listen to what they say and how they say it.

Respond with:

> *"I hear you, but according to Federal law, namely the Civil Rights Act and Fair Housing Act, no one involved in real estate sales is allowed to discuss the ethnic, racial or age make-up of any particular neighborhood because to do so would be a violation of those Federal Laws. I'm sure you understand. By the way . . ."*

Go back into your presentation of the home's features and benefits.

The best practice here is to give all customers full information on all areas where they are qualified to buy, and let those customers make the decision on their own.

"Let your customers get to know you first before ever talking about real estate."

Chapter 6

HOW BELIEFS AFFECT
NEW HOME PURCHASES

It's useful to find out early if multicultural customers have beliefs that might affect their purchase of a new home. Ask questions as you would of any potential home buyer about colors, floor plans, or how many bedrooms and bathrooms they require. It's just as important to know about the preferences of people from other cultures as it is those of your own.

You may want to show your new home buyers this book to indicate that you have more than a passing interest in meeting the needs of other cultures. You might say, "This book discusses cultural beliefs and practices that may influence the purchase of a new home. Is it possible that you might have any that would affect which model or floor plan you choose?" Most multicultural customers truly appreciate this kind of question and will go out of their way to explain their cultural beliefs.

It's certainly true that some cultures have virtually no convictions that might influence the purchase of real estate, while others have whole systems of applicable rituals. For instance, Middle Easterners, Pakistanis and Haitians tend to prefer single-story homes, but that is many times the extent of cultural impact. On the other hand, some Asian groups have deeply held religious beliefs that influence the direction an acceptable home faces, where it is located on a street and how it is designed.

FENG SHUI

Some Chinese believe in *Feng Shui* (pronounced "fung show-way"), literally "wind and water." It is an entire system of beliefs on the role of natural harmony, especially the placement of buildings. It prescribes, among other things, that the stove and sink must not be placed opposite each other because fire and water do not mix or that doors should open inward instead of outward so that good luck does not leave the home. A stairway should not lead directly to the front door because it allows good luck to leave the home easily.

Feng Shui also teaches that bad luck travels in straight lines. It says that these lines create "secret arrows" along which negative energy or "chi" luck travels in curved patterns. On the other hand, good luck travels in curved paths. Thus, for those who believe strongly, a curved or spiral staircase would be preferred over a straight one and round windows over rectangular. The author has consulted with home builders who were trying to appeal to Asian home buyers and demonstrated how they could make a bad luck straight walkway into a lucky curved one with just a few extra pounds of cement. Another way is to use round windows instead of all rectangular, or even triangular ones, to change negative energy into positive.

Believers in *Feng Shui* do not like homes situated at a "T-intersection" (see diagram). You can see why—the bad luck traveling down a street on secret arrows can enter the home without impediment. This could also be true to a lesser degree for the homes on either side or at the end of a cul-de-sac.

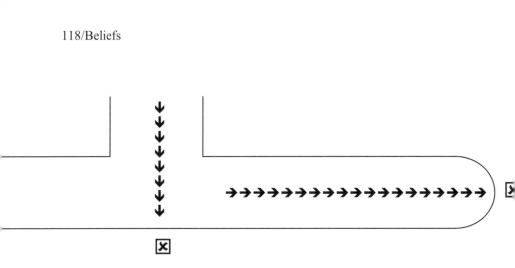

The beliefs of Feng Shui are too numerous and wide-ranging to put in any book in fullest detail. Ultimately, the only way you will know what your particular customers believe in is by asking them. This book is meant to be your head start at knowing what to ask, why and how.

Death in the home is another significant topic for Asian home buyers. Again, some Asians believe that a former owner's good or bad fortune foretells the kind of luck subsequent owners are likely to experience. For this reason, many Asians prefer new homes since they cannot have a history of bad luck for the owners. (Most Americans also prefer a home without any negative history; just ask the sales representative who tries to rent or sell a property that has been the scene of a notorious crime.) On the other hand, a home with a previous owner who won the state lottery might well bring a premium price from some buyers with this belief.

Asians have a particular aversion to homes with histories of untimely or violent death, such as murder or suicide. Such a background is believed to induce bad luck. Even if they plan to rent out the property, some shrink at the thought that bad fortune may follow the rental money back to the owner. In China, those who believe the tenets of "predecessor death" will often burn a home to the ground to free the evil spirits within.

Japanese followers of traditional culture will avoid buying a home where a murder, suicide, foreclosure or similar catastrophic event has caused the sale of the home. They believe that it is wrong to gain advantage from others' misfortunes.

For the average American new home buyer, having a cemetery in plain sight of the home is not overly objectionable. In fact, many new home sales representatives are fond of joking, "You'll never hear any noise from those neighbors." However, in the minds of Chinese who believe in *Feng Shui* those secret arrows will travel from the grave site to your home and make your property unlucky.

Yet, for almost every bad-luck secret arrow there is a counter-measure to nullify it if your customer is willing to go to the trouble of implementing it. The careful placement of a mirror, rock, tree or water fountain can absorb, deflect or reflect secret arrows. However, a believer in *Feng Shui* will only be willing to go to the trouble of finding and implementing a counter-measure if the home is perceived to be a good enough value to warrant the effort. Instead of trying to solve the cause of bad energy, your time would be better spent showing buyers how homes in your community have appreciated in price, if appropriate.

VASTU SHASTRA

Feng Shui is not the only belief system that can affect home choice. In India, ancient principles called *Vastu Shastra* are said to promote happiness and prosperity. According to *Vastu*, the home should be surrounded by a wall at a greater distance from the home on the east and north sides. *Vastu* also dictates that the building should be at least three feet above road level and oriented toward the cardinal points of the compass. This belief seems to have a practical explanation given the history of annual monsoons in India.

Vastu Shastra prescribes that the main entrance (front door) be the largest, and the exit door (back door) the smallest to keep the good luck in the home. The center of the building is supposed to be free of beams, pillars or columns. Ideally, the north and east sides of the home open onto verandahs.

Vastu also says valuables such as important documents, money and jewelry should be placed in the corner of the southwest portion of the home and face toward the north. The southeast is for the kitchen, to position the cook toward the sacred east while meals are being prepared. The sink should stand in the east or northeast side of the kitchen.

The master bedroom should be located in the southwest or *Niruthi* of the home. The occupants should sleep in the southwest corner of the room with their heads to the south. Beds must not touch the walls of this room. The west side of the home is for the children's rooms, with the beds on the southwest side so their heads face toward the west.

Many Indians want a separate room to be set aside as a prayer room. It should face the east and not open up to a bathroom. Some developers have successfully converted laundry rooms for this purpose while moving the laundry facilities to the garage.

The room in the northeast corner is called the *Puja* room.

It is believed that medicines stored here will develop enhanced healing properties. The northwest part of the home is for incidental use, like garages, guest rooms, toilets and storage. The garage should not be in front of the home or it will block good luck.

On the south and west sides of the property, deciduous trees like guava or coconut are recommended. Windows and plenty of light are encouraged but the total area of openings on the north and east sides are supposed to exceed that of the south and west. Finally, staircases can be in the west, south, southwest, or southeast sides. The top step of each should angle either to the south or the west.

Obviously, the complexity of this belief dictates that the only real way to know what your customers believe is to ask them directly. The earlier you find out that a customer subscribes to this or any other similar belief, the better off you will be. It will give you more time to adjust and make allowances.

HOME ORIENTATION

You can see how Asian Indians are quite concerned about the direction the home faces. So, too, are other groups like the Chinese. Some believe like the Indians that a home should face to the east. Others, Koreans for instance, prefer south-facing homes like those in their cold native land to take advantage of maximum sunlight throughout the day. Many Chinese do not want the front door to face north because ancient folklore says this is where the devil lives—with his home on a direct line of sight, he can certainly see yours and send bad luck your way.

In the same way, some Japanese like eastern or southern

exposure to fit the weather patterns of their home country. They prefer that the headboard in the master bedroom not be on the north wall—they bury their dead facing that direction.

People from India tend to like east-facing homes. They also like pie-shaped home sites that are narrow in front and wide in the back, or what they call *gaumukhi* or "cow." Many dislike the opposite orientation with a wide front and narrow rear, called *shermukhi* or "lion."

HISPANIC PREFERENCES

Hispanics don't harbor many beliefs that relate to the home, but some features tend to be more attractive to members of this culture. A large, well-equipped kitchen is a major selling point for Hispanic women. When showing a home with an outstanding kitchen to a woman from this culture, let her view that room first. They also like well-appointed bathrooms.

A few culturally unique appointments might include tile roofs, earthen-colored tile on the kitchen floor, arched doorways and natural wood as opposed to painted. Hispanics may also prefer green or red tile on the counter.

A lack of fixed ideas notwithstanding, Hispanics can be very particular about their housing needs. Home ownership is very important, but they don't seem to like condominiums or townhomes because they seem more like apartments than houses. They like the freedom of being able to do what they want with the home instead of being restricted by landlords or protective covenants.

In addition, attractive grounds, prized in this culture, are usually small or nonexistent in multiple family buildings.

Hispanic families may even prefer a smaller single-family home to a larger condo or townhome located in an otherwise more appealing neighborhood.

Like their Latino brethren, Hispanics may look for homes with more bedrooms and bathrooms because of the common practice of inviting extended family and valued friends to stay with them. Therefore, given the ability to qualify, four or five bedrooms and three to four baths would be preferred over smaller homes.

Be sure not to add custom features that are "culturally unique" until the sale is assured. Putting in red tile on the kitchen counters, red carpets or other amenities might make it difficult to sell the home to other buyers if a transaction falls apart.

Remember, it is quite common to involve extended family in the purchase of a new home. Be prepared to deal with not only the immediate family purchasing the home, but also with brothers, sisters, in-laws, grandparents and even godparents who often provide part or all of the initial deposit.

The eldest son or daughter in a Hispanic family may be present to speak for the interests of the younger children in real estate transactions. Give this family member respect and let him or her handle the papers like any other person involved in the transaction.

Hispanics are inclined to be more fatalistic, perhaps from the influence of the Catholic Church. Americans, a majority of whom are Protestant, tend to believe they have a partnership with God and therefore have control over their own success. Many Hispanics subscribe to the belief that their destiny is in God's hands alone, and there is little they can do but make the most of it. A wise sales representative will avoid such philosophical differences during negotiations.

For generations 80% of the land in Mexico has been owned by only two percent of the people, the upper and ruling class whose ancestral home lies in Spain. The "average" Mexicans, the *Mestizos* (mixed blood) and *Indios* (Mayan Indian stock) are not accustomed to owning land in their home country, but it is certainly a major goal for those coming here. It may be the chief reason for many. Owning a new home is an instant sign of success in America for people from this culture.

For similar reasons, Koreans coming to America want to own real estate. For centuries, only a handful of powerful families have held almost all of the land there. The opportunity to own real estate in the U.S. is a major goal for Koreans. Like Hispanics, a new home says instantly that they have "made it" in this country to friends and family back home.

Because of their unfamiliarity with the new home buying process and construction, you must go extremely slowly when explaining the details. Your patience will reward you with loyalty for a lifetime.

NUMEROLOGY

Belief in numerology can also affect the choice of a new home. A superstitious reliance on numbers is certainly not intrinsic to new immigrants alone. Many Americans would not want to be treated on the 13th floor of a hospital; most hotels and many office buildings in this country conveniently deleted this floor number.

The author happened to be riding in an elevator of a high-rise hotel one day with several Japanese nationals. As we watched the floor indicators jump from the 12th to the 14th floor they asked me why. Initially they thought it must be some restricted club level. I explained that, in America, people believe that the number 13 is unlucky, so we simply ignore it when numbering our floors. I recall them making some remark about how superstitious Americans are!

There is probably no culture on earth lacking in curious beliefs about numbers. In many Asian countries the number eight is considered lucky, while four is unlucky. In Chinese dialects, these numbers are "homophones:" The word for "eight" (*baat*) sounds like their word for "rich" or "luck," which is also pronounced *baat,* but with a different emphasis. "Four" (*sei*) sounds like their word for "death" (*se-i*).

Likewise, the Japanese word for "four" sounds exactly like their word for "death," and the word for "nine" sounds like the word for "suffering." As a result there are few hotels or hospitals in that country that designate its floors or rooms with those numbers.

Koreans' lucky numbers are three and seven, while the number four is unlucky for similar reasons as in China. In Korean the number "four" is pronounced *sa,* while death is also *sa.* Why other Asian cultures whose languages are different have similar beliefs is lost in history, but may be related to longtime contact with the Chinese, Japanese and Koreans.

Those who believe in numerological precepts follow it very strongly. For example, A wealthy gentleman in Hong Kong paid over $1.5 million for the personalized automobile license plate "88888" which he took to mean "rich-rich-rich-rich-rich." Think before laughing about this seemingly frivolous purchase. First, where did he get such a large sum of money? Could it be because of his belief in numerology in the first place? Also, just imagine for how much he might later sell the plate to another believer! It would be unwise to make light of this common belief in the power of numbers. Think how many people in this country who scoff at numerology would have the money to purchase such a plate.

Nevertheless, not every Asian group believes the number four unlucky. Many Filipinos believe that the quantity "three" is equally unlucky. In fact, some are convinced that three steps leading to a front door signify inescapable misfortune. Others believe that any multiple of three is a bad sign. This stems from the Filipino adage *oro, plata, mata*, meaning that the first step leading to a home represents gold, or *oro*, the second step silver, or *plata*, and the third step death, or *mata*. It is not unusual to see Filipino new home customers meticulously counting steps and subsequently making the decision to buy or not buy a property based on this belief.

In contrast to others, many Filipinos believe the number seven or eight to be lucky or *suerte*. Former President Ferdinand Marcos ruled the country for over 20 years carefully following the dictates of the number seven. One who asked him even a simple question could almost count on Marcos taking seven minutes, hours or days to respond. He also usually wrote laws consisting of seven parts.

Numerology affects the purchase of real estate in many ways. Homes with addresses like "444" or "4444" will probably not sell to Asians who believe that these numbers signify triple or quadruple death. Building departments where significant numbers of people believe in numerology have been besieged by requests for address changes. Some authorities have turned this belief to their profit by agreeing to an address change for a fee, as long as it does not disrupt the logical sequence of homes. As a practical solution, adding an eight or another lucky number can remedy the reputed bad luck brought by a given address.

If a new home salesperson has a potential customer who likes everything about a home except its "bad luck" address, and that address cannot be changed by local authorities, there is one last option. You can look at the "Lot and Block" or Assessor's Parcel Number of the parcel they are interested in. If it is either a neutral or a positive number, you can explain to the buyers that this is the "official address" (it actually is, according to the county assessor) and that the address on the home is only used for mail delivery.

Some savvy new home builders attempt to attract believers in numerology by eliminating the number four in the asking price, using eight in its place. A price like "$108,888" may indicate that this tactic has been applied. The same marketing ploy has always been used to attract Americans who believe in the number seven, as in "$107,777;" it has just been adjusted for the latest group of new immigrants.

People from India may consult astrological calendars for good and bad auspices. This practice is recommended by Rahu Kalam, a belief system based on the negative influence of the planet Rahu. Inauspicious days and hours are: Mondays from 7:30 to 9:00 AM; Saturdays from 9:00 to 10:30 AM; Fridays from 10:30 to Noon; Wednesdays from Noon to 1:30 PM; Thursdays from 1:30 to 3:00 PM; Tuesdays from 3:00 to 4:30 PM and Sundays from 4:30 to 6:00 PM. People who believe in these 90-minute increments remember it by the mnemonic device, "Mother Saw Father Wearing The Turban on Sunday."

New home salespeople, therefore, need to be aware that Eastern Indians may not be available for appointments during these hours.

Again, many people who profess a strong belief in numerology may modify their faith if they like the home enough or think it is a good bargain. The author has seen staunch followers of numerology purchase a home they really wanted having the address "1142," despite the fact that it contained a "4," and the numbers added up to "8."

PETS

Pets present difficulties for some multicultural buyers. Dogs and cats are domesticated in American culture, but in parts of the world like the Philippines and Southeast Asia they are sources of food. Listen attentively to your customers as you get to know them. When they have them, Asians generally prefer pets that emit little or no odor, like fish or birds.

For instance, Filipinos and other Asian cultures, like Southeast Asians, don't like the smells of domestic animals in the home any more than Americans like the odor of chickens or pigs. If you are a big animal lover you should probably forgo any discussion about your pet-of-choice when talking to customers from other cultures, unless they express an interest first.

In the Middle East, dogs are used for hunting and for watchdogs but are not kept in the home. In fact, to call someone in that country a "dog" is to imply that they are a dirty, low form of life.

If you are in the habit of bringing your dog to work, it can present other problems. Dogs, for example, are not domesticated in many other countries. Most Americans have never been attacked by a pack of vicious wild dogs, a common experience in some places. If you sense fear or hesitancy, take this to mean your customers do not like pets. Better to leave your pet at home if you have a large number of multicultural customers in your community.

COLORS

Color takes on different meanings in different cultures. Asians tend to avoid pure white homes, as that color is associated with death. For the same reason, snow-white chrysanthemums are given to the mourners at Asian funerals. For people from Peru, Mexico or Iran, yellow flowers have a similar meaning. Red means good luck for the Chinese, while the same color means death for Koreans. For this reason never sign a Korean's name in red or hand them a red pen with which to sign their name; this act would imply that you wished them dead. Red is also the color of mourning for people in Ghana.

In the Western societies, black is the color of mourning, while white is worn to weddings, but in many Asian countries it may be just the opposite. In China, for instance, white is worn to funerals, and black is the attire for weddings.

In Japan, the color purple is believed to fade fastest, so never wear this color to a happy event like a wedding or a birthday party. It implies that you hope the happiness of the event is short-lived.

The Philippines presents an exception to the Asian aversion to the color white. They, like Westerners, believe that black is the symbol of death.

PLANTS AND TREES

Some cultures are very concerned about plants and trees. The Chinese, for example, will use trees to block bad energy from entering the home. Koreans may want to preserve as many trees on the home site as possible. For them trees are sacred because when the Japanese invaded their country many years ago, the invaders cut down all the trees to build ships for the Royal Japanese Navy. Also, cutting the trees was a psychological sign of subjugation. This was so traumatic to the Koreans that even today, there is a national holiday called "Tree Day" on which people plant trees. You may want to let the buyers physically tag the trees they want to preserve on their home sites; that helps them to "own" the purchase.

After reading about other peoples' beliefs, I think you can see that they really aren't quite so unique or hard to understand. In fact, you may have similar beliefs even though you are not from another culture or recently immigrated.

If you recognize the fact that every group of people, including your own, have beliefs, people from other cultures wouldn't seem so difficult to understand. This is the first step to breaking down barriers to rapport and building a lifetime relationship with your customers, their friends and family.

CONSECRATION

Other cultures frequently have special ways of christening the new home. Many cultural groups want to conduct a consecration ceremony before construction begins on a new home. The dictionary defines "consecration" as "to dedicate" or "to set apart as holy."

The biggest question in regards to this issue is, "When does construction begin in their minds?" If the buyers want to conduct a consecration ceremony it is vitally important to determine the exact point at which the buyers want to have this done.

Some groups may want to have the ground blessed before leveling of the land or trenching begins for the foundation. This will usually consist of having a priest, minister or some other religious representative conduct a ceremony asking for good luck and harmony to reside in this place. It's an interesting sight to watch construction workers sitting on bulldozers gazing in amazement at the blessing rite before they can begin their work. Others may bring a live animal to sacrifice on the land before work begins. You can see that you will want to know the exact details of the ceremony so you can check that they don't violate any laws, sensibilities or sensitivities.

Other people may prefer to wait until the foundation is ready to be poured to have the ground blessed. A common practice during such a ceremony is to place objects of significance into the cement as the foundation is poured. Objects such as money are supposed to bring good fortune to the inhabitants.

Given these practices, it's important to ask every new home buyer if they have any desire to consecrate the site before construction and at what point they would like to do this. Otherwise, you will miss the opportunity to let them enjoy this part of their belief, and many buyers will not purchase a new home they have not had the chance to bless in their own way.

Obviously, the time frame for consecration should be placed into the construction calendar just like any other critical part of the building process. The author has witnessed many new home sales fall apart after the buyers arrive with their religious representative to consecrate the ground, only to find that it has already been broken by careless construction workers unaware of the buyers' wishes and its significance.

By the way, this practice is not so unusual among Americans who like to place representative objects in time capsules in the foundations of buildings. Catholics also like to bury statues of St. Joseph face down in the front yard for good luck.

Just keep in mind the importance of the consecration ceremony to some groups. Remember to ask if they have such a desire and at what point they want it to take place. As in any successful sales transaction, what is important to the customer should be important to the builder and all who represent him or her.

So, ask your customers if there will be some sort of ceremony and ask if it would be fitting for you to participate. You will probably find it interesting and enlightening.

"Every culture has beliefs – we need to learn about any beliefs our customers hold that will affect the new home purchase."

Chapter 7
WRITING THE PURCHASE AGREEMENT

Purchase agreements can present one of the most frustrating parts of the real estate transaction when dealing with people from other cultures. The author has personally witnessed and has had countless new home salespeople complain about how "unethical" certain groups of people appear because they continue to negotiate after a purchase agreement has been signed.

Are people from other cultures really unethical, or are they just different? To answer this question, several things must be understood about writing a purchase agreement for a customer from another country. Remember that the United States is a "low context" country, meaning that we rely on words to express our thoughts. This leads us to place everything we intend into a very wordy and lengthy purchase agreement. This is why American purchase agreements are so complex. Everything from purchase price to closing date to the inspections are placed into the purchase agreement so that there will be no confusion as to what was agreed upon.

As an example of the complexity of agreements in this country, think about how detailed the builder's contract is with its subcontractors. Everything from the size of the nails to the quality of the wood used is specified in writing.

In "high context" countries such as Mexico, China and Japan, much more is implied and less is "spelled out." In some countries, such as in the Middle East, to have too many details in a purchase agreement implies mistrust between the parties. In places like Asia, it is understood that the purchase agreement is the starting point of a relationship and an agreement that will necessarily change over time to suit the needs of both parties. It is expected that when one party needs to adjust the terms, the other party will actively help change the purchase agreement.

In the United States, we believe that signing a purchase agreement means the end of all negotiations and bargaining. In countries like China, a purchase agreement could be taken as the first step in a period during which the terms, conditions and price are open to further discussion and change. Do you see how easily confusion and charges of unethical behavior could naturally develop out of the different ways countries view purchase agreements? It has nothing to do with ethics or the lack thereof; it's just a different way of handling the contractual relationship.

The author has heard hundreds of new home salespeople across the country lamenting that they couldn't understand why some Asian customers tried to stretch out the negotiations after the purchase agreement was signed, even after close of escrow and final passage of title. These salespeople didn't know that these customers' culture taught them to view signing a purchase agreement as the opening of negotiations – not the end.

Another area of confusion for American new home professionals is the "ridiculously low" offers on purchase prices that many people from other cultures will make in spite of the fact that they are constantly told that the price of a new home is non-negotiable. These low initial prices could serve to anger the builder, resulting in a total rejection of the purchase agreement or, at best, full price or higher counter offers.

While the United States is essentially a non-negotiating country, in most countries negotiation is a practical and essential art. Through a long and drawn-out process the participants get to know one another and, hopefully, build a long-term relationship that will make future relations much more efficient. In these places, it is not unusual to start the haggling at what American sales representatives would consider a ridiculously low starting price. Why not? This is a relationship building process and the foundation of any solid building begins at the very bottom.

New home salespeople must understand that most multicultural customers are quite willing to pay a realistic price, but feel gypped without the opportunity to negotiate. Therefore, their thinking is that you cannot have much of a chance to negotiate if you start near the asking price.

Some builders refuse to negotiate the price of a new home since it could devalue all of the previously sold homes in the area. New home buyers have won lawsuits when they claimed that their home lost value because the builder subsequently sold homes at a discount.

The best way to handle multicultural new home buyers who feel they must negotiate is to write up any purchase agreement they feel appropriate and then present it to the builder. In all likelihood it will be rejected, but the way it is explained to the customer is crucial. After giving the buyer the opportunity to negotiate, you should tell them, "The builder has sold all the other homes in the neighborhood at this price. To save face with those other buyers, he must sell you this home at the same price."

Most people from other cultures understand the concept of "saving face" which implies the opposite of losing honor. This is probably the best technique for countering the tactic of people who feel they must negotiate the price of a new home. It's just a different way to explain the "Checkerboard Pricing" technique.

Checkerboard pricing is a term created by Bob Schultz that refers to the condition that results when a community has different values on homes that should have similar values, creating a "checkerboard" effect, which is ultimately bad for all concerned. Bob explains that you would be upset if you found out that your neighbors all paid less for their new homes than you did.

Another issue that new home salespeople often face is nearby competitors who might regularly and openly negotiate their prices. One of the best ways to handle this practice is simply to ask, "You know, I wonder how they do that? We don't have to discount our homes." This immediately implies that your homes are of higher quality, and quality definitely motivates new home buyers.

The following SST^{SM} from Bob Schultz's *Smart Selling Techniques*^{SM} is another strategy to employ when you are in this situation.

SITUATION

The customer states the "competition" is making better deals.

STRATEGY

To communicate that a deal may not be in the customer's best interest.

SST-SMART SELLING℠ TECHNIQUE

"I am sure you are like most customers who are looking for the best value. Many times what appears to be a great price may be just an illusion. We at (name of your company) build value into our homes through quality, amenities and personal satisfaction. I would welcome the opportunity to assist you in making the comparisons and perhaps you will find as many others have that our homes are even a better value than you imagined."

Once the purchase agreement is signed, conflict between cultures can really become evident. You can try reminding new home customers that in the United States, when they sign the purchase agreement and the seller accepts, this ends the negotiations. You want to be blunt with people like your pre-approved Jamaican customers and let them know that "unless you drop dead, you must complete the transaction as you have agreed." Some builders will take buyers to court to enforce the terms of the agreement if anyone, regardless of culture, tries to re-negotiate the purchase agreement after it has been signed. Many buyers from other countries do not take seriously threats of legal action when they try to change the deal after signing. Their experience of the legal system in their home country, which may be even slower and less effective than the U.S. judicial system, leads them to believe that such threats are hollow and without force.

It's much more effective to plan ahead for some people's tendency to renegotiate the purchase agreement than it is to threaten or even follow-through on a lawsuit. If you know that many people, including some Americans, are going to ask for more during the transaction, be sure not to give them everything you are willing to throw in at the beginning of the transaction. Good negotiators know that they have the most leverage just before the deal closes, so that is when you save your best negotiating chip.

New home buyers from negotiating countries consider it a mark of honor to obtain something extra at the close of escrow. They may ask for landscaping, an automatic garage door opener, upgraded carpet or anything else they think they can get. It is immaterial to most of these buyers what they actually end up with, but it is important that they receive something extra to demonstrate their negotiating abilities to friends and family.

Some developers with whom the author has worked have experienced such a consistent problem with renegotiation that they have built into the purchase price a little something extra to counter this tendency. If the salesperson does not succumb to the tactic, they get to keep part of the "closing incentive." Don't forget that the tradition of negotiating is thousands of years old and almost impossible to break.

Try to provide copies of the purchase agreement as far in advance of signing as possible. Remember that the American government did not treat the ancestors of many people from other countries kindly, so there may be a reluctance and fear of signing government-looking documents.

The author gives every buyer with whom he chooses to work a written guide that explains the entire home buying process and includes a sample copy of the purchase agreement. This guide is provided at the very first meeting to build credibility and provide value to the customer. It also gives the customer an opportunity to review the purchase agreement at their leisure and ask questions throughout the home buying process. Having had a copy of the agreement in their possession for so long, it doesn't seem as imposing as when they first see it at the time they must commit to a purchase.

Providing a sample purchase agreement in advance also enables buyers to obtain a translation in their native language and have it explained by someone familiar with real estate transactions. Remember that the English language can be difficult and confusing for people from other countries to understand. Add to this the complexities of American real estate and contract law and you have a potentially frightening document, one that few people in this country understand.

Spend some time with your buyers early in the home buying process to explain each line of the purchase agreement and what it means to them. Again, this gives them the opportunity to ask questions or obtain outside clarification. You will probably want to keep a bilingual dictionary handy, preferably one that specializes in real estate terms. These are available at most major bookstores. A written explanation of the basic home building process would be greatly appreciated by any new home buyer, regardless of culture.

Before writing the purchase agreement, show your customers what other buyers are paying for comparable properties in the area. You may be able to show them that the values of your properties are rising after each phase has been sold out. This helps your buyers understand the value of the property on which they are about to write a purchase agreement. Remember, some have come from countries where the prices could be less than one-quarter of what they are being asked to offer. Is it any wonder they want to start low?

There is another fact that all good negotiators know – the asking price sets the absolute upper limit of what the seller thinks their property is worth. A buyer can never go down, only up from whatever initial price he or she makes. Therefore, why not start low and let the seller work you up from there?

Regardless of how attractive the initial price is that the new home buyer makes, the builder should always make a counter-offer. Otherwise, the buyer will think he or she paid too much. Unless they are clear on the value they are receiving, they could feel that the price is too high.

Some home preferences of new immigrants are not specifically culture-related. For instance, many prefer gated communities because of the security and sense of community that these neighborhoods provide. From the earliest history of the United States, immigrants have taken the blame for problems such as unemployment and depressions. Today's new arrivals are no different, as newspapers carry stories of violence against Asians, Hispanics, Middle-Easterners and others. Gated communities offer a haven from their fears of street violence. Don't be surprised if they express a preference for these.

African Americans like their homes to look different and unique. It's probably best not to mention the "traditional look" of your homes or communities. Remember that for this group, American tradition does not hold the best of memories.

With African Americans, more than any other group, you should carefully explain the reasons for any rules or policies. If they think they are not being applied equally to all new home buyers, they will likely feel discriminated against. For instance, one couple from this group wanted a relatively unique brick facade applied to the front of their new home, but company policy forbade any two adjoining homes from having similar looking architectural styles to avoid the "tract look." Unfortunately, this policy wasn't explained at the very beginning of the new home buying process, and the buyers of the home next door already had requested the same brick. The customers believed that this rule was invented only after they had decided on the brick to keep them from getting what they wanted.

The resulting conflict could have been avoided if the policy had been explained earlier and if the salesperson had realized that the buyers just wanted to make their home look different from the others. There were several other options that would have accomplished this same goal if they had only been offered.

All else aside, don't allow the customer whose primary language is not English to become so dependent upon you that they don't read the purchase agreement. You certainly don't want them just to sign anything you tell them to. Have a relative or friend who is bilingual in the customer's language and in English translate everything before they obligate themselves to the biggest purchase of their lives. You do not want to end up trying to tell a judge and jury why you did not bring in a translator to render a complicated legal document intelligible to the customers.

Treat customers as you would want to be treated. In their place, you would want to be sure you understood every finest detail before committing yourself to a new home purchase. It's called The Golden Rule, and it is a very good policy to apply with all your customers.

"Different cultures view purchase agreements differently. In America we put everything in writing. In other countries being too specific implies mistrust."

Chapter 8

NEGOTIATING

Just mention the word "negotiate" and some of the most experienced new home salespeople can break out in a cold sweat. Say the words "multicultural negotiations," and many will run screaming from the sales office.

Remember that there are two types of countries in the world – negotiating and non-negotiating. Except for two big-ticket purchases, the United States is a non-negotiating country. Those items are cars and houses, and Americans really dislike negotiating them both. We are so uncomfortable with negotiating in this country that the Saturn car company catapulted into popularity by providing a reliable car at a fixed price. This "no-haggle" method of purchasing an automobile became so attractive that even a mega-car maker like General Motors has selectively instituted a form of it in its "Value Pricing" policy.

This leaves real estate as the last true bastion of negotiating in America. It's also usually the largest purchase anyone could ever make, further increasing the tension and discomfort with the process dramatically.

Most other countries around the world are negotiating countries where, outside of the major metropolitan areas, people negotiate for everything from groceries to laundry services to rent. They have become masters of dickering simply by living in these locations. Don't forget that in some of these countries the standard of living is much lower, so every dollar that can be saved through sharp negotiating is crucial to survival.

In America, vendors have agreed to set prices with no

negotiating in mind, so that the time spent in this activity is minimized. Remember, in the United States "time is money." However, in other countries, time is used to build relationships, and negotiating is a way that two parties can get to know one another. It is as much a part of the socialization process in foreign countries as cocktail parties are in America.

Much of the confusion and frustration that new home salespeople feel when dealing with people from other cultures centers around this issue of negotiation. Let's look at some of the differences.

The first difference between how we in the United States and those from other countries negotiate is speed. Here we like to get down to business, and "get it over with" right away. In Asia or Latin America, negotiations proceed at what seems to us in this country to be an excruciatingly slow pace. The author did some negotiations in Japan in which he attended five consecutive customer meetings during which the business at hand never came up. It wasn't until we had built a relationship over lunches of sushi (raw fish) and sake (rice wine) did negotiations finally begin.

In Argentina, it may take a number of trips to reach agreement simply because several people—some of whom won't attend most of the meetings—must approve each decision. This is a very standard negotiating tactic that we in this country call relying on "The Higher Authority." Just like at American new car dealerships, no one Argentine negotiator seems to have the power to completely ratify the purchase agreement.

Negotiations might also move at a slower pace than Americans are accustomed to because other cultures use the early stages to develop the relationship between the parties. We use it to determine bargaining positions. Others anticipate negotiations with delight and genuinely enjoy them. They feel that getting acquainted with the other party is just as important as closing a deal.

Each culture has its own unique negotiating style. In South Korea, for example, they may ask a question over and over. Koreans are by no means dumb, but rather, are trying to explore all options to be sure they are making the right choice. In Japan, it is important to say, "I'm sorry" during negotiations as a sign of politeness. Expect Germans to be direct and businesslike, even abrupt, in negotiations. People from Israel are very confrontational and emotional in their negotiating style, which can intimidate Americans. In Saudi Arabia and Egypt, they will come physically very close during negotiations and often touch the other party, which we here view as being too aggressive.

Another difference in negotiations between cultures is in the weight and importance attached to issues. Americans habitually concentrate on the immediate substantive matters like price, quality or availability, while Japanese, for example, are more concerned with the quality of the people they are doing business with—in building a lifetime relationship.

Trust is crucial if a negotiation is going to be ultimately successful in the eyes of all parties. But different cultural groups establish trust in different ways. Some look to past experience, others rely on intuition and emotion, and still others count on rules that assure performance.

Americans tend to rely on the past history and reputation of those with whom they negotiate, while the Japanese are more concerned about the nature of the relationship they are building with the other party. To many cultures, especially Asian cultures, solid personal relationships help minimize potential social conflict.

People from negotiating countries take great pride in their bargaining ability. If they think they are overpaying, they will do just about anything to kill the deal, regardless of how beneficial to them you honestly believe it is.

No matter how much the builder is tempted to accept the purchase agreement without any kind of counter, it is still imperative that you convince them to make some small change. If the deal is going to disintegrate, it's better to let it happen early than at close of escrow when everyone has invested tremendous amounts of time and energy.

This is the standard negotiating tactic of "covering your bottom line," building in something to compensate the buyer just in case the price was too high for the property. After all, your customers are probably somewhat new to the country and may not be completely familiar with new home values in the area. In all likelihood, they are paying a great deal more for a home in the United States than they would in their home country.

Among the many techniques of master negotiators is "nibbling," the ploy of asking for previously unmentioned small items as if they have just come to mind. Because of the relief and almost euphoric atmosphere that follows successful negotiations, this technique is especially effective immediately after the parties have come to an agreement. Nibbling could take the form of asking for upgrades or any of an infinite number of other concessions. As with big requests dealt with earlier, nibbling must be stopped in its tracks or there will be no end to it.

To stop constant requests for more and more, make it a rule to ask the buyer for a concession before ever giving one. For instance, if a customer says, "We would like to extend escrow by two weeks," respond with, "What will you do for us in return for extending escrow? Would you pay the builder's carrying costs and property taxes for that period? It would be an expense that we haven't anticipated, you know." Once your buyers understand that every demand they make will bring a similar demand from the builder, they will stop asking.

Some cultural groups are less flexible than others are. Filipinos and some others of Asian origin may adopt a "take-it-or-leave-it" stance. You may be able to forestall this prospect by approaching the subject in the rapport-building stages. Explain simply, without direct reference to the customers, that this ploy is often a deal-killer in this country.

If you don't explain carefully everything you do to help customers and how little you actually make, your commission will quickly become the subject of negotiation. It's worth a few minutes to detail these facts at the beginning of your relationship. Fail to discuss it early, and many hours may have to be invested defending your compensation to someone who is committed to getting a piece of it for themselves. If negotiations begin with a multicultural buyer believing that his or her salesperson does nothing, only to earn an exorbitant amount of money, you can be sure that your commission will become fair game for negotiation.

Again, people from other cultures tend to be effective negotiators. They almost always start with a very low offering price. This is particularly true for Chinese and Jamaicans. However, build good rapport and they will look to you as a friend and not just a salesperson. Point out the benefits of the home, then present a menu of offering prices: Low—you will probably not even get a counter-offer from the builder; Medium—you will probably get a significant counter-offer; High—you will likely get the purchase agreement accepted with very little counter-offer. Find out how badly they want the new home and set the purchase price accordingly.

If you are in a sellers' market and the buyer persists in making low starting purchase prices, even when several purchase agreements are being submitted on the property, you may wish to refer them to another community (perhaps your biggest competitor). Until the market changes, many people from negotiating countries will not understand why they should make purchase agreements at or above asking price. You may waste a great deal of time if they won't adjust to the market.

It's probably not a good idea to tell the developer the cultural background of the buyer because it might give them an opportunity to discriminate. Again, just explain that your buyers like to bargain. By the way, who doesn't?

Presenting purchase agreements for multicultural buyers in a sellers' market can be frustrating, especially when there are already multiple purchase agreements, some even above the asking price. However, when your buyers see comparables showing the value of the property and know that others are making purchase agreements, they will usually become more reasonable. If not competently and completely explained, the vital process of educating people from negotiating cultures is frustrating for many new home salespeople.

Counteroffers should be provided to any new home buyer regardless of cultural background or how high the initial purchase price. The key point, again, is that if the purchase agreement is accepted as originally presented, they may believe they are paying too much and try to back out.

If, for some reason, the builder insists on accepting your buyer's purchase agreement as written (usually for fear of losing them), please don't rush back to your customers with the "good news." Take your time and carefully explain how hard you worked to get them to accept the purchase agreement without changes, in spite of the fact that they didn't want to. What seller doesn't want a higher sales price or to keep most of their personal property?

Some cultural groups are quite fatalistic about negotiations. When the builder rejects their purchase agreement, some Hispanics say, "God must have preordained it." With the same meaning, Pakistanis would say, "Life goes on." This attitude of not getting emotionally involved makes some multicultural prospects tough on salespeople who are unaccustomed to playing the game this way.

In fact, some Chinese simply will not allow themselves to become emotionally involved over the purchase of a new home. It is only an investment; if they don't buy the property they are currently writing a purchase agreement on, another will surely come along.

Japanese sellers often close their eyes during negotiations as a way to concentrate on what the other side is saying or has proposed. The ensuing long periods of silence will often drive Americans crazy, but it should not be broken until the seller breaks it. Take comfort in knowing that when they do this, they are not withdrawing from the conversation. Rather, they are listening intently and considering every word.

The Japanese home buyers will rarely say "no," even if they disagree. Just because they don't say "no" does not necessarily mean "yes." There are definite signs that Japanese do not agree with what is said, such as stating, "This is very difficult," or impatiently sucking air through their teeth.

The Japanese hate to say "no" so much that they have developed at least 16 ways to avoid saying the word. Indonesians are similarly disposed and have 12 different ways to avoid saying "no."

Even the Aboriginal people of central Australia are rather unassertive people who like to avoid direct confrontation. They avoid having to say "no" by putting off discussions with which they might disagree.

Arabs rarely say "no" because it is considered in this culture to be impolite. There is an old saying that when an Arab says "yes," he means maybe. When he says "maybe," he means no. Instead of "no," an Arab may often say, "if God is willing."

The Chinese can drive people who don't understand their methods of negotiation nearly to distraction. This cultural group takes its time as they try to wear down the other side. Or, they may delay responding as a way to kill the deal without losing face.

Koreans customarily try to delay with a complicated panoply of contrived excuses. They often make the opposing side wait until the last minute for an answer. On the other hand, Koreans are the most likely of all the Asian groups to give a "no" response. They tend to be more direct than most other people from the Far East are.

Because they do it every day, people from negotiating countries have become masters of the art. To them, it is as natural as breathing. This apparent effortlessness is one of the reasons it drives new home salespeople here so crazy. However, if Americans could observe how multicultural people negotiate with an open mind, we just might learn a few techniques that could save our customers and us a great deal of money.

"Most cultures negotiate everything everyday--
America is one of the few countries that does not
regularly negotiate. We must learn to do
it better."

Chapter 9

WORKING WITH AFFILIATED PROFESSIONS

People in related professions like loan officers, title and escrow persons, various inspectors, attorneys and subcontractors can help or hinder you. The lender is one of the first people your buyers will meet (unless they are paying all cash). This makes it essential to send them to a competent and understanding bank, mortgage company or loan broker.

Give your lender the correct pronunciation of your clients' names, and note which is the husband and which is the wife, if applicable. All of the trouble you went through to get an unusual name correct could be totally wasted if it isn't communicated to everyone who will be dealing with the customers.

Even if you are using an in-house or "captive" lender, give them your résumé and encourage him or her to tell the customers something specific from it about you in the first few minutes of the relationship. People from other countries rely heavily on such word-of-mouth. A few brief words like, "Oh, you're Michael Lee's customers. Do you know that he's got a son who's an honor student?" or "Did you know that Michael Lee is a private pilot?" These few words can buy you years of trust and loyalty and a gold mine of referrals from multicultural customers.

Have your co-professionals make you real to your customers by saying something about you that is not related to real estate. Such facts like the number of children you have, any hobbies you engage in, languages other than English that you speak make you more human instead of just a "salesperson."

Take the effort to make sure that every real estate-related company mentions some detail from your biography. It's clear that people from any culture connect better to a person who is known and respected by others than they ever would to a corporation. The reference should include both professional and personal information.

Vietnamese and Hispanics in particular may join together with members of their own culture to help one another buy homes. You must build a list of lenders who understand and will work with this kind of pooling. They should be aware that many multicultural groups, Hispanics and others, are first-time home buyers as a rule, so every step of the transaction must be explained thoroughly and carefully.

For other reasons, Middle-Eastern people may not want to obtain financing from a Middle-Eastern bank or have someone of similar descent represent the lender. Again, the level of mistrust they might hold for others of their culture makes this necessary.

There is probably no procedure equivalent to the title search in your buyers' home country. In some parts of this country a title company does the job, while in others it falls to an attorney. No matter who performs this important task, it's critical for you to impress upon the buyers the importance of guaranteeing them a clear title to the property.

If you elect to use an attorney's services, explain his or her function in the real estate transaction to the customer. In some countries—Great Britain is one—attorneys earn their respect, while in some other countries anyone can call himself a lawyer by simply hanging out an impressive sign. On the possibility that the buyers come from one of the latter countries, it's up to you to ensure that they have confidence in this participant in the transaction.

Some new home developers use neutral escrow companies to hold funds for the seller and to transfer title to the buyer. The United States is fairly unique in this practice, so a clear explanation of the escrow function should be given to any buyer. Most escrow companies have a brochure available explaining their duties and the steps required to closing escrow.

Nearly every bank requires some minimum amount of fire insurance to protect their securing interest while some also require liability insurance before providing a loan. In a number of cultures, merely talking about potential catastrophes is tantamount to issuing an invitation for fires, floods and earthquakes to destroy the home. Carefully explain to your customers the importance of insurance before they run unprepared into the issue.

Several kinds of inspections are available or required in different parts of the country. The necessity for such inspections as roof, pest control, well water, structural, septic tank, geologic, toxic waste, soils and others as appropriate in your area should be explained to buyers. These may or may not be first-time home buyers, but they are probably unfamiliar with our language, customs and laws. New home salespeople are even more responsible for detailing the material facts for new immigrants than they would be to people who are more familiar with our customs.

As with any first-time home buyer, you should inform people from other countries that they should expect to hear some bad news from any inspector. It's their job to find flaws and point them out, even in a new home. Let your customers know that flaws do not necessarily mean that the home is about to fall down, but you will discuss the implications of any inspection reports as they come in.

Carefully explain to any first-time home buyer who the people are on your real estate "team" and how they help buyers to own the new home of their dreams. These players might include decoration, design, finance, job site foreman, building coordination, landscaping, etc. You should stress that real estate is a difficult profession that requires the services of many specialists to assure a sound purchase. Let the buyer know that it is your job to coordinate all of these people and make sure all necessary documents are provided as required.

Do not give your buyers, especially those from other countries, unrealistic expectations about costs or deadlines. Otherwise, if things cost more than you estimated, or take longer than you thought, they will assume you have lied. This can ruin an entire relationship for a few dollars or a few days. Always give yourself a cushion so that things cost less and are completed quicker than you estimate. This way you look like a genius and will win the confidence of all your customers.

Remember that the decorator and construction people are an integral part of the new home transaction. The decorator and foreman should also be given the correct pronunciation of the buyers' names, and it should be noted which is the husband and which is the wife.

The decorator should make it clear to the buyer that he or she is a salaried employee of the builder's and has limited ability to change the purchase agreement from the way it is written. Good negotiators will try to use anyone remotely connected with the transaction to better their position, if they can.

Construction people should also try to be sensitive to the needs of new home buyers. Some groups may believe that because they are minorities, they are being treated less equitably than other buyers are. Carpenters, plumbers, electricians and other tradespeople must be aware that they may be asked to prove that the quality of materials being used is the same for everyone. They must be patient and slowly explain the construction process and not become angry with the buyers.

Accidents or loud arguing can taint the building site in the eyes of some buyers. Construction foremen must train their people to be careful and sensitive to the needs of all buyers.

"The job of the new home salesperson is to coordinate all of the people needed to put together a transaction."

Chapter 10

WORKING WITH
MULTICULTURAL HOME SELLERS

Some buyers will have to sell their present home before they can invest in a new home in your community. As more and more people from other cultures buy homes in America, they will eventually become sellers. Culture continues its impact when they take the opposite role. The familiarity with the process that they acquired when they bought the property is incomplete at best. It now must be complemented with knowledge of "the other side's" part in things.

Some developers refer buyers with a home to sell to an in-house resale brokerage firm, a group of selected resale agents or companies. Be familiar with your builder's policy in regard to this issue.

Some developers are willing to accept purchase agreements on new homes contingent upon the successful sale of a current property. You should know what your builder's policy is regarding accepting contingent purchase agreements.

Some developers have their own resale companies just to handle this possibility. They know that the more control they have over the entire transaction, the more likely they are to sell the buyers a new home.

As with buyers, the first area in which culture affects the real estate transaction is in picking a resale agent to sell the home. If chosen, you must assume the agent who originally sold them the property did not explain everything professionals do on behalf of sellers; if he or she did, you are ahead of the game. Still, make it a point to tell them how little you really get paid from each sale or you may encounter that common tendency for these sellers to ask for part of your commission.

This is the first discussion you should have with a seller of any culture. As you do with buyers, deal with the common sellers' myth of overpaid, do-nothing agents at the first opportunity. Show them a list of things that you do to help them sell their home.

The next area of selling affected by culture is the important action of "staging" the property for maximum appeal. The owners may like colors and furniture a majority of buyers are likely to find unattractive. Explain that if they want the best price they must prepare the property for sale. They need to know that most buyers find neutral colors and a minimum of traditional furniture more attractive. Tell them that it makes it easier for the buyers to visualize the changes they will make to fit the home to their tastes and lifestyles, as the sellers undoubtedly did after they bought it.

Another issue you will likely have to address is the offering price. Just as people from bargaining countries like to pay the least possible price when they buy, they want to get the most when they sell. As a result, some of your multicultural sellers may ask you to list their properties well over the real value of comparable properties. It is imperative that you explain to them that a home that sits on the market for an inordinately long time may actually bring a lower price. Potential buyers and other sales representatives may begin to fear that something undisclosed must be wrong with it.

If they still insist on an unrealistically high listing price, suggest they seek the services of another representative. Let them understand that it simply isn't worth your time and it's a waste of your professional skills trying to sell an unrealistically priced property. Another factor: The real estate profession does not need more "OPTs" (over-priced turkeys) on the market to give sales representatives an even worse image than we already undeservedly have.

Some multicultural groups are more concerned about the

offering price than the terms and conditions. It is important to many Saudis, for instance, to sell the property as close as they can to their asking price. This is evidence of business acumen in their culture. This fact makes it still more important to set the listing price at a realistic level.

Still another sensitive issue is whether or not to leave things in the home that indicate that the owner came from another culture. Maximizing value for the seller should be a major concern of every listing sales representative. If that means removing some furniture or taking family photos off the wall, you must bring up the subject confidently. The Wall Street Journal has printed several articles about how some listing sales representatives suggest that African American customers make their homes "culturally neutral" to bring the highest price. Personal considerations aside, every real estate professional must know the market and make appropriate judgments on this issue.

You will need to carefully explain to multicultural sellers the need to know their loan balance and account number in order to assure smooth payoff of this loan. Remember that people from other countries can be very private about these and other issues.

Being good negotiators, multicultural sellers who are going to be listing their home with you and buying another through you will very often ask for a discount on the listing commission and possibly a kickback on the purchase side. It's important to explain that you will do just as much work on these two transactions as you would working with two individual customers.

If you do decide to give your current seller/future buyer a discount because you might have increased efficiencies working with one party for two transactions, the author suggests that you not give the discount on the listing commission. If you give any concessions it should probably be on the purchase of their next home through you. Otherwise, you may find that you have discounted your fee to a break-even point hoping to make it up on their next transaction, only to discover they have bought through someone else. It's not unusual for buyers to walk into a for-sale-by-owner or different new home community. Or they might suddenly remember a friend or relative in the real estate business. By only giving the concession on the purchase of the next home, you are providing substantial inducement to stick with you as their sales representative and buy in your neighborhood.

Especially if multicultural buyers make an offer on your listing, suggest that the sellers not include everything, such as personal property, that they are willing to give at the first sight of a purchase agreement. Sellers from most other cultures will have little difficulty understanding and agreeing to prevent reopened purchase agreement negotiations days before close of escrow. Decide in advance which negotiable items the seller will hold back until just before close of escrow.

"Multicultural sellers must be educated about what real estate professionals do for a living and how much they make."

Chapter 11
MARKETING TO MULTICULTURAL CUSTOMERS

There are marketing issues of which you should be aware if you want to attract new immigrant customers to your new home community. First, people from other cultures don't customarily find new homes through general circulation newspapers or Yellow Pages advertising. As a rule, they prefer to receive a reference from trusted friends and relatives.

It is vital to ask your current multicultural customers for the names of anyone they know who might be thinking of buying a new home. It is equally important to get them to introduce you personally, since this is a very crucial part of the trust building phase. Ideally, they should speak positively about you to the reference before they introduce you. (More on this in Chapter 14.)

You may decide to advertise in newspapers and various other media that serve the interests of diverse cultures. However, know that if a different language is spoken and your ad is written in that tongue, potential customers are probably going to expect you to speak it. Developers who don't have multilingual salespeople ought not to try using this strategy.

Advertising in the United States is "low context," meaning that people from this culture rely on words to explain a product and its features. Other cultures that are low context include North America, Switzerland and Germany.

High context cultures like those found in most Asian and Latin American countries, as well as the Native American culture, rely more on pictures and nuances to convey meaning.

These cultures find low context ads and techniques to be "pushy and aggressive." The saying, "A picture is worth a thousand words," really epitomizes the preferred method of marketing to this group. This is a good reason to do less talking when speaking to people from high-context cultures as well.

Recognize that you cannot market to all groups in the same way. You must find out how the groups you are trying to reach receive their information and reach them through these media.

To people from other cultures, traditional ads that feature European Americans are virtually invisible. Use appropriate models and language for the group you are trying to reach.

Don't forget that the dominant religion of the Middle East is Islam. Do not use any symbols or words in your advertising that imply Judeo-Christian values. Things such as stars, crosses or even asterisks may be taken the wrong way by such readers.

Eighty percent of Hispanics listen to Spanish-speaking radio stations, and 75% watch Spanish television. This group is fiercely loyal to their language and culture and prefer that their ads be in Spanish.

Hispanics are very brand conscious and loyal to leading brands. If your real estate company is a member of a large nationwide franchise, you may wish to stress this attribute to buyers from this group. On the other hand, members of this culture are very family oriented, and if your company is family owned and operated you may prefer to mention this feature.

It's a little-known fact that 70% of Hispanics believe Christopher Columbus to be a beloved figure in their culture. Using his image would certainly not hurt identity with their group.

Hispanics also tend to read direct mail more than any other group. While most people often throw away anything that appears to be "junk mail," Hispanics rarely receive such mailings and are more likely to read them.

A majority of Asians seem to prefer to read newspapers for their information as opposed to radio and television. Do not make emotional appeals to this group such as, "You'll love this home." Remember, Asians consider it poor taste to display emotions in public, and they do not respond to emotional pitches.

To appeal to Asians, stress the longevity, reputation, quality and reliability of you and your company. Saying "new and improved" is not attractive to people from a 5,000-year-old culture.

It's important not to knock your competition when marketing or working with Asians. They believe that if you do so, the person who makes negative comments is the one who loses face. Instead, stress the benefits and strengths of your company.

To Japanese customers, don't say that your company or neighborhood is "distinctive" or "unique." Remember they value group harmony and fitting in. The Japanese have a saying that epitomizes this philosophy: "The nail that sticks up gets hammered down." Asians want to conform and work with companies that are team players.

If you stress time savings to Koreans, you will have their undying loyalty. Many regularly work 14-16 hours a day and six to seven days a week. Time is at a premium, and they often wish they could spend more time with their family, especially the children. Emphasize dishwashers, garbage disposals and microwave ovens that all help to save time, as does a location close to shopping and transportation. Don't forget that some people from other countries are not used to these modern appliances, and it may take a great deal of time and patience to explain their proper usage.

Many Koreans and Eastern Indians work for high technology companies in the United States. Thus, it may be possible to market to them using a web site or e-mail.

Asian Indians often have large families and prefer companies with a family orientation. While they are usually very westernized and speak English, you should use Indian models and show a family in your ads. As a bonus, many Indian/English language newspapers are relatively inexpensive to advertise in.

It's important to remember that African Americans are not just dark-skinned people, but ones with a separate and distinct culture. This is why they have developed their own newspapers, radio and television stations to meet their unique needs.

Seventy percent of African Americans read Black community newspapers. Use models from this culture and be careful when showing what you may believe to be traditional families. Remember that a majority of these families do not have a male as the head of the household.

When marketing your real estate company to African Americans, de-emphasize size and longevity. Large, impersonal companies and governments have historically treated this group very badly. They prefer to work with small, personalized, entrepreneurial sales representatives and companies.

Many African Americans do not like things that appear as or imply traditional values. These kinds of values have been used against them since their ancestors were brought over from Africa as slaves. They like to express their own unique style when it comes to home ownership. They also tend to like distinctively styled homes that stand out from the rest.

Certain words are particularly attractive to multicultural people, words like "family," security, "prestige" or others that describe desirable features. But stay out of trouble by verifying with your advertising outlet that some perfectly innocent words do not inadvertently violate Fair Housing or anti-discrimination laws. A little personal research with members of the ethnic communities you hope to work with can go a long way, too.

Many people come here from places where it was not unusual for a family business to operate in the same place for generations. If your business is long established—at least 10 years, preferably longer—you may wish to suggest trustworthiness by featuring the fact. The mindset you are aiming to address is the conception that it is unlikely that your business could have lasted so long by cheating people. Also stress the family aspect of your company, if appropriate.

Be careful when using coupon offers to new immigrants or even long-time Americans like African Americans and Native Americans. These are very self-sufficient cultures and don't like anything that looks like food stamps or welfare.

Keep in mind the significance of colors to some cultural groups. For example, consider red ink or red paper when advertising to Chinese; in their culture, that color represents good luck and prosperity. Don't forget that this is the color of death for Koreans.

Always have someone fluent in the language of the people you are trying to reach double-check your ad for any mistakes or cultural gaffes. Some companies who ought to have known better suffered great embarrassments they could have avoided with better planning.

Stories are told about Pepsi-Cola executives who had a hard time understanding why sales were slow when the company first began distributing its product in Taiwan. In time, someone explained that their slogan "Pepsi brings good things to life" had been mistranslated into Chinese to say "Pepsi brings your ancestors back from the dead." Those who weren't amused might have been offended, since ancestors are the subjects of reverence in that culture. The result of Pepsi's miscalculation was more than embarrassing. It was a potential disaster for both sales and public relations.

Because of a similar error in translation, it is said that the management at General Motors was sorely disappointed when its popular Chevrolet Nova line flopped miserably in Mexico and South America. They had believed their compact model, so popular here, couldn't miss in that new market. Sales projections were very optimistic when the campaign kicked off, but actual sales were disappointing. Eventually, a kind soul made them aware that the name "nova," which Americans associate with a shooting star, sounded like the Spanish phrase *no va*, meaning "It doesn't go." In both cases millions of dollars in promotional costs were wasted because no one did his cultural homework.

Until you are confident in your ability with ethnic differences, find your own "expert" to confirm that you are taking an acceptable approach. It's not a good idea to try saving a few bucks with the high school Spanish you learned 20 years ago.

"You must market to multicultural customers in the way they want to be reached."

Chapter 12

USING INTERPRETERS AND TRANSLATORS

Real estate words and concepts may need a specialist to convert them to English. Few countries outside the Unites States feature title and escrow systems and other real estate-specific services. Important as they are here, such functions require skill and patience to explain. Be prepared to handle the ethnic and cultural diversities you encounter with three things: empathy, patience and understanding.

One language cannot always be accurately translated into another. In fact, it can often become an impossible task because some words can have no meaning outside of their specific culture.

Employing interpreters and translators is a common business practice of sales representatives working with unfamiliar cultures. Interpreters convert the spoken word to English, while translators deal with the written word. If possible, find one with real estate experience. Whatever the cost, good ones will be worth considerably more than what you pay them.

An extra benefit is that an interpreter gives you additional time to consider your response in negotiations. So it is of some importance for your interpreter to understand your goals in the transaction. The purpose is to meet those goals, so brief anyone you hire in advance to explain the nature of the deal and the part you expect them to play.

Locating a competent and experienced interpreter or translator can be crucial to your success. Colleagues or customers with whom you completed good property transactions should be your first source. You might also want to contact the nearest consular office for the appropriate country.

It can be disastrous to accept the first person who applies; a poor interpreter can create irreparable catastrophes. It is legendary that when former President Jimmy Carter visited Poland in 1977, his interpreter butchered his official arrival message. When he said that he had left the United States early that day, the translator told those assembled that Carter had "abandoned" his country. When the religious Carter talked about Polish "desires for the future," it was translated as their "lusts for the future." As if that wasn't bad enough, the interpreter ended the address saying, "The President says he is pleased to be here in Poland grasping your secret parts."

The interpretation of American-style English is difficult. Our language is filled with colloquialisms, acronyms, idioms, slang and jargon. Add to this the special requirements of technical real estate terms, and the task can be just about impossible for an inexperienced interpreter. A bad job can easily lead to misunderstandings and even lawsuits. Once you have selected a candidate or two, hand them a few documents and ask him or her to explain them. Even though your knowledge of the language may be poor, your expertise in real estate can help avoid mistakes in this regard.

Using an interpreter effectively requires the establishment of three-way rapport between yourself and the interpreter, between yourself and your customer and between the interpreter and the customer. This takes time and should be taken into account when planning your meeting using an interpreter.

Explain any technical terms you will be using to your interpreter. Ask them to explain any cultural differences in eye contact or other nonverbal issues that will affect your meeting. Ask about any local customs such as the most appropriate time for a meeting, the customer's concept of time and any appropriate factors.

Once everyone is together, speak directly to your guests, not to your interpreter. Speaking to the interpreter and not the clients would be seen as rude. It is helpful to practice a few simple signals with your interpreter so that he or she can let you know when you're speaking too quickly or slowly. Since it's easy to lose control of the conversation when using a surrogate, agree on other signs—you'll probably not use them—that would signal to your employee about something you might want to inject into the dialogue. Before meeting with the customers, practice speaking in short phrases and pausing from time to time so your interpreter can catch up.

Never, never try to tell jokes through an interpreter. It rarely works well and can be disastrous if not done just right. A story or subject that is perfectly acceptable in our culture could well offend people from another. Or just as bad, it might not be funny in a different language.

Recognize that direct translation of English into other languages is often impossible. Too many words have more than one meaning, and may have unexpected connotations in other tongues. Common real estate terms may have no direct equivalent. And of course, cultural orientation itself can have an impact on the translation. Despite the help an interpreter can provide, it's still a good idea to draw diagrams and write figures down as if there were no one else there.

Salespeople who have used interpreters know from experience that it will increase the time needed for communications. Plan for that when you allocate the time for a meeting with multicultural customers. Don't be shy about telling them why the meeting may be a long one. "I want to be sure to communicate everything so we all understand, so I'm going to allow for the extra time we will need for three people to talk."

Interpreting is a difficult and taxing job, both mentally and physically. That's true even for the most experienced professional. Provide your interpreter with lots of water and snacks, as well as plenty of breaks. Again, don't shrink from telling the customer exactly why.

Treat your interpreter with consideration since clients often look at how we treat our colleagues and assume they will be treated the same way. Your first consideration after his or her competence level is to employ an interpreter with whom you are comfortable and feel can work effectively with you as a team. The person you choose should behave in a like manner as you do in such personality characteristics as aggressiveness, friendliness and shyness. In this way every word will be consistent with your own style. Be sure the dialect of the interpreter is the same as the people with whom you have hired him or her to communicate. Chinese, for example, is a language with hundreds of dialects, all classified in the West as Chinese but sometimes incomprehensible to one another.

Once more for emphasis, take the necessary time to hire someone with real estate experience, someone who knows the unique terminology of the profession. It may cost more, or it may not, but in any case the dividends of choosing someone who is as professional at his or her job as you are at yours will be great.

"Try to find an interpreter who has real estate experience."

Chapter 13

OBTAINING REFERRALS FROM CUSTOMERS

Once you have served a multicultural new home customer well, the word will spread, and you will probably acquire more. As mentioned, the bulk of immigrants find service providers who are sensitive to their needs by word-of-mouth. You will never have a deeper business relationship than one in which you have both educated a customer and been educated by them.

The Saudi Arabian reliance on the recommendations of friends, for instance, comes from centuries of trust in personal contacts that saw them through periods of drought in their desert homeland. Asians feel so strongly in referrals that they will personally introduce their friends and family to a new home salesperson. Hispanics treat a trusted businessperson as a member of the family.

It is always a good idea to give every customer a gift at closing. The author has given every conceivable present during 20 years in real estate. My list of gifts to new homeowners ranges from door knockers to cookie jars and everything between. After spending thousands of dollars on small remembrances, I've concluded that an effective closing gift should accomplish only one goal: It regularly reminds the customers that I am their salesperson for life. A gift that doesn't satisfy this paramount requirement is a waste of money.

The best closing gifts come with personalized plaques and are appropriate to the property involved in the transaction. A business gift suits the sale of an office building, as a household item fits in the new home. Such things as pen and pencil desk sets and similar items are ideal. My most effective closing gift is a glass and brass clock that spins every few seconds. I put a matching brass plate at the base reading, "Congratulations on your new home, from your friend, Michael Lee." Beneath that inscription I put the date of closing. The wonderful thing about the clock is that the customers are reminded of me every time they glance at it, dust it off or change the battery.

However, the gift of a clock would be extremely inappropriate to some groups of people. Remember that they remind the Chinese of the winding down of life or of funerals. Clearly, the Chinese consider receiving a clock in itself an unlucky event. I give such customers the pen and pencil set with the same brass plate.

It is also in poor taste to give knives or scissors to a Chinese or Japanese because they stand for the severing of a relationship. As explained earlier, you should never give most Asians four of anything or Filipinos three of anything, as those quantities remind them of death.

Another good closing gift for people from the Asian culture is a green houseplant wrapped with a red ribbon. Green symbolizes growth and life, while the red is for luck. Remember to omit the red ribbon for Koreans.

I like to give my Japanese customers a small gift at the first meeting and another at close of escrow. These customers are likewise probably going want to give you presents on these occasions. To stress the point once more, it is crucial never to outspend a Japanese customer. Your mistake will cause them to lose face and never be able to speak to you again.

Wrapping paper is another unexpected closing gifts issue. Never wrap a gift for a Chinese or Japanese in white paper.

Again, white is the color of death in both lands. The Japanese culture passes out chrysanthemums at a funeral, and everyone at a funeral wears white. Also, the Japanese consider brightly colored paper and fancy ribbons in bad taste. If you ever look for wrapping paper at a Japanese stationery store, you'll find it very subdued. Chinese, on the other hand, frequently wrap their presents in red, their culture's color of good luck and happiness.

A strong, small tree is a good closing gift for Koreans. Remember that this group has a great affinity and affection for trees.

Food baskets, crystal glass items and fine liquor are all excellent gifts for Chinese and Japanese customers. Unfortunately, I haven't found a way to personalize any of these. The problem with gifts that do not lend themselves to plaques is that, if there is no reminder attached, the giver tends to pass from memory rather quickly, especially if not a family member. Haven't you ever received a gift and then forgotten who gave it to you?

Whatever gift you give your multicultural customers be certain it is of the highest quality and is not imported from their own home country. You want to welcome them to America, not give them something they could have easily purchased at home and probably for less money. Nothing but humiliation could result from a Japanese customer's turning over a fine piece of crystal only to read "Made in Japan." To give a Hispanic, an Arab, or anyone new to America a gift made in the place they just left would certainly not remind them of their new home in America.

Good house warming gifts for Japanese might be high quality liquor such as Scotch or Brandy. A word of warning on liquor is appropriate: Regardless of quality, nothing alcoholic must ever be given to anyone of a religion such as Islam, which frowns on all alcoholic beverages.

When you exchange gifts with Japanese, present yours with both hands like the business card, extend it forward with your left hand, and receive their gift to you with your right. At the other end of the gift-giving conventions, Muslims never pass or receive anything with the left hand. It pays to give attention to the receiver as well as the gift.

You may find that your Japanese, Chinese and Mexican customers are extremely loyal and will almost automatically refer friends and family. These cultures place a high importance on loyalty. Gratitude also carries value as evidence of good quality and worthy purpose, so be sure to acknowledge the favor of a good referral in an appropriate manner.

However, you must consistently ask for referrals, otherwise most people will not remember to refer you. The best time to ask for a referral is anytime a customer expresses gratitude. If they say, "Thank you, I never thought we could afford to buy a new home!" simply reply, "You're certainly welcome. Is there anyone you know who might also like to acquire a new home?"

Remember that the way the multicultural new home buyers find a trusted builder is through referrals, so they want to refer you. Give them the opportunity!

Providing a referral means several things to your customer: 1) It's somewhat of an ego boost for them to know more than their friends do about new homes, and this is their chance to help them find a trustworthy salesperson and builder; 2) They can help others with a referral; and 3) They pay you back for all of your services by referring a friend or family member.

The way you accept a reference is crucial to your success with referrals. When a customer gives you a referral you need to say, "Thank you, Ahmed, I promise I will call them right after you tell them about me." Then when you call the referred party say, "I promised <u>Ahmed</u> I would call you." Isn't this better than saying, "<u>Ahmed</u> gave me your name"? Stated in this manner, this is a sacred promise you have kept. It starts your relationship off in a very positive manner.

"People from other cultures want to make referrals – give them the opportunity to refer you."

Chapter 14

CLOSING THE TRANSACTION

As an experienced new home salesperson, you know it is good practice to keep all your buyers and sellers up to date on the progress of the transaction. The most common complaint heard about real estate sales representatives across the nation is "They don't stay in touch." That's especially true during the final stages when close of escrow is pending. In new home sales this is often one of the busiest times when finishing work is being completed, inspections are being done and new home orientations are being conducted.

A weekly phone call is probably about right, but it's helpful to determine how often they would like you to contact them in your very first meeting. A daily call may not be sufficient during the busy completion stage of a new home.

The biggest fear of listing agents is having to call their sellers to tell them that nothing is happening with their property. Far worse, though, is for them to call you anxiously, only to learn that nothing is happening. The conventional wisdom is that that scenario is a sure-fire recipe to a disgruntled seller. But an even worse scenario is the one with a nervous seller sitting at home imagining all manner of disasters. Even when you have little or nothing to report, make it a point to stay in touch regularly.

Don't lull yourself into a false sense of security from the relaxed atmosphere projected by some cultures. It practically never lasts. A typical Jamaican customer may be weeks late in providing the documents needed to close. Later on, that same apparently lackadaisical person may wear your ear to a nub with repeated phone calls demanding to know why nothing is happening. If such is the case, remind him that nothing is ever going to happen until the necessary papers have been provided. It is close to impossible to over-communicate with a customer.

Do not expect people from other cultures to blithely sign a stack of official-looking documents without some reluctance. Even to someone from this country, that mountain of papers can be quite imposing; this is doubly so to persons who are unfamiliar with the American language and culture. It's also significant that certain peoples have not had good experiences with the U.S. government in previous times; bad past experience just increases their occasional reluctance to sign official-looking documents.

Be sensitive about presenting closing documents to people from the African American or Native American cultures. Their long history of poor treatment by some, part of which can be attributed to the U.S. government, leads them to be careful about what they sign.

For similar historical reasons, Asians are not always trusting of the paperwork necessary to transfer property. They have their own history of maltreatment at the hands of earlier American government policymakers. On the other hand, studies show that members of the Hispanic culture are twice as likely as European Americans are to trust the government.

The best way to handing the huge pile of closing documents that both buyers and sellers must sign is to arrange to obtain a *pro forma* set from the title company or attorney well in advance of closing. Give customers from other countries at least a week in advance to review all papers before expecting them to sign. Explain anything that might be a concern. Also alert them to the fact that on the day of closing they will be expected to sign papers rather quickly, so now is the best time to look everything over and ask questions.

Some Filipino buyers will want to close escrow and move on a full moon. This can be tricky, especially when the full moon falls on a weekend. One way the author has handled this problem is to explain that once everyone signs the papers, the buyers own the home for all intents and purposes. At that point, recording the title is only a legal formality.

Other buyers such as Indians and Chinese also have lucky and unlucky days. The sooner you discover this fact, the more time you have to plan ahead.

Expect new Filipino homeowners to bring a full sack of rice and some salt or garlic to their new home. Tradition dictates that they do so for luck before moving anything else in the door. That ritual accomplished, a priest will give his blessing upon the new family abode.

"Providing closing documents in advance and staying in touch will win the undying gratitude of your buyers."

CONCLUSION

Remember that immigrants are having a tremendous impact on new home construction in America. The one million people coming into the country annually help assure the health of our $800 billion industry.

There's a very good reason why new immigrants are so important to builders. New homes can be especially attractive to members of some cultures. Many Asians might prefer a brand new property because there are no previous owners who might have suffered ill fortune. Hispanics might favor new properties because the rooms may be larger than in older homes. African Americans can customize them so they reflect their own unique style. In fact, almost every culture would probably prefer a new home to a used one if price and location were no object.

Besides, what other accomplishment of a new immigrant says you have achieved success in your new homeland than purchasing a brand new home? What would make their family back home prouder than sending them a picture of him or her in front of a new American home?

However, new homes can be troublesome to people from countries where negotiating is common. Most new home developers will not negotiate the price because doing so could lower the value of all of the other homes in the area for which the owners paid a higher price. The way to overcome this obstacle is to explain to your customers, especially Asians, that in order for the developer to "save face" with the previous buyers, the purchase price must remain fixed. Nonetheless, upgrades or other amenities obtained as part of the deal may enable you to show the customer how you helped reduce the net purchase price with each "upgrade."

Almost all developers allocate their salespeople a "discretionary fund" ranging anywhere from a few hundred to thousands of dollars that gives them some flexibility in making a sale. The amount varies depending on the price range of the home, how long the community has been marketing a particular set of properties, the builder's profit margin, etc. Developers are reminded <u>not</u> to give them everything up front, otherwise should renegotiation become a factor, you will have nothing left to give. When the author consults with home builders, he shows them how to build in a "renegotiation factor" into their discretionary funds so the salespeople cannot give it all away at the beginning.

New home builders and developers should be aware of the influence immigrant groups can have on their business. The best sources of information regarding the wants and needs of people from other cultures are the builders' own salespeople who interface with customers all day long. If multicultural customers begin having a large impact on sales, developers may want to consider planning properties to satisfy these customers' needs.

Again, many Asians prefer that the walkway leading to the home be slightly curved rather than straight; straight walks are believed to create "secret arrows" that provide a path for bad luck. They may also favor round windows over the trendy triangular ones because triangles represent three straight lines of negative energy. Practitioners of *Feng Shui* will prefer certain home orientation, room layouts and appliance placement, as previously discussed. Don't forget the rules of *Vastu Shastra* for Asian Indian customers who subscribe to this belief.

One of the most requested options for people from other

cultures seems to be to vent the kitchen exhaust outside the home. Far too many developers today simply vent cooking odors back into the kitchen to save money. People who cook a lot of fish or use strong spices know the smell stays in the home for a long time, sometimes permanently, so these customers often want the air blown outside by a strong fan surrounded by a large hood over the range.

Another popular feature in new homes is the "granny unit" option, which substitutes a smaller bedroom with a bath in place of a library room. Many people from other countries expect to have friends and relatives stay over when they visit.

The author has consulted with many new home developers and shown them how simple, inexpensive changes can make their properties much more attractive to their unique customers. The best way to know what your specific customers prefer is to ask them. Have your salespeople regularly survey the market as most new home developers do, adding such questions to the usual as: "What color exterior do you prefer?" "What changes in layout would you suggest?" "How do the appliances suit your needs?" "Any other suggestions?"

One of the difficulties that home builders have is getting their sales force to have model home visitors complete surveys. These forms provide valuable information, as well as vital contact data for future follow-up. This problem is rather easy to understand because salespeople believe correctly that they get paid to sell, not to get questionnaires filled out. But this information is too valuable not to obtain, so new home representatives need to be rewarded for obtaining it.

One developer brings balloons filled with various denominations of bills hidden inside to the weekly sales meeting.

Salespeople who have turned in more than a certain number of completed surveys get to pop them against a dart board. For each extra completed survey, the person gets one dart. This game adds amusement to the meetings, and the developer gets valuable and needed information on prospects. Balloons usually contain lots of $1 and $5 bills, some $20's, a few $50's and one $100 bill. The balloon popping ceremony is usually the highlight of the meeting and encourages other salespeople to obtain completed survey cards.

Developers should ask salespeople if visitors regularly request custom features that the developer does not provide. If a sufficient number of requests come in, perhaps the developer should consider adding them.

In general, multicultural home buyers tend to prefer things they are familiar with from their native country. Many Jamaicans, for example, like block and steel construction as is common in their homeland. They often ask builders to use concrete blocks between rooms instead of the sheet rock found in most construction here. This gives them a greater feeling of security against inclement weather, like the hurricanes that are familiar to those who have lived in Jamaica.

Some new home buyers demonstrate unusual (to us) taste in color and style. Red is thought lucky for some Asians, so crimson or plum colored carpeting might be preferred. However, as not all buyers like this color, builders should be careful not to install such unusual decor until the sale is pretty well assured. Many developers have found themselves with difficulty trying to resell new homes with custom features that made it difficult to find a new buyer.

If a new community is heavily impacted by multicultural

home buyers, everyone in the selling firm must be made aware of the special needs of such customers. It is well to set aside specific training time for the sales force to learn about special needs, interests, and requests that might affect the selling and escrow processes.

For instance, many immigrants who invest in a new home like to visit the site to watch their home being built. If they hear loud arguing between the workers, they may conclude that this will be a home filled with discord and disharmony. It might have a similar effect if there is a serious accident during construction. How the developer handles these and other issues affecting multicultural buyers is crucial.

Remember that the multicultural buyer may want to consecrate the ground before construction begins. Be sure to coordinate this with their religious representative before any work is begun like trenching or pouring foundation. If this opportunity is lost, so might be the sale.

Everyone who works for a new home developer can be affected by cultural differences and should be aware of this fact. Not only the salespeople on the front line, but also decorators, carpenters, people in finance and all other tradespeople can help determine the success a project has with its potential multicultural market.

The first thing that should be done by salespeople is to get the customers' names correct. As noted earlier, be sure to get the spelling and pronunciation right, along with the family name (surname). When sending this information on to other people within the company, give them a phonetic pronunciation and note which is the husband and which is the wife. It's very embarrassing to call a customer's workplace asking for a man and a woman answers. This small mistake makes the entire company seem callous and uncaring.

The next thing new home salespeople should do is explain what they do for a living and how much they make. This is as vital in new home sales as it is in resales because many buyers, culture aside, think that new home salespeople are the same as resale agents. Another myth about resale agents that also is commonly believed about new home salespeople is that salespeople do very little to earn a huge amount of money. You do not need to tell the buyer exactly how much you make, but give them a percentage of the sales price. Don't forget to deduct your income taxes and expenses so that they can compare your take-home pay to theirs.

Next, explain the new home model touring procedure. Many new home buyers, regardless of culture, do not know how to tour a new home or that the model furniture is not included.

Point out any custom features that might be of interest, and explain what can and cannot be done. Many new home buyers think that all builders can totally customize a home or build it on the home site of their choice somewhere else in the area.

New homes can be a tremendous opportunity to help multicultural buyers own the ultimate American dream. However, as you can see, you must adjust your thinking and practices to do so.

I trust you will take the information about new home buyers I have compiled for you in this book and put it to work. I believe you will find that working with people from unfamiliar cultures an enjoyable and beneficial experience. They can become your most loyal customers and best teachers.

Obviously, you cannot remember everything in this book. The good news is that you don't need to. All you really need to learn is what is important to your customers regardless of what country or culture they come from. Through this book, you now have the tools to begin your studies. You are going to become the multicultural expert in your area by keeping an open mind and asking natural questions that come up because you are truly interested in learning about other people.

Never forget that you are fulfilling the dream of a lifetime for new immigrants – owning a brand new American home. They also want what everyone else in this country wants: to live in neighborhoods where they can raise their families in safety and harmony. They want their children to attend the best schools possible, and they want those children to have the greatest chance at success in the United States.

Remember that every person you meet in the new home sales profession is an individual with rights, interests and visions of the future that are their own, yet much like everyone else's. Understanding their cultures and beliefs will help you to establish friendship, rapport, and sound business success.

If nothing else, don't assume a customer wants to be treated in a certain way. Take time to know the culture your customer comes from. Then learn what changes have taken place in the customer since coming here. You may be surprised. Be sensitive to cultural differences, and it will pay you personal and professional dividends.

If ever you are in doubt how to act or what to say around multicultural customers, you could follow the Golden Rule follow the "traditional" Golden Rule. *Treat all buyers as you would like to be treated*, with sensitivity, patience and a desire to serve them with the best that is in you. Taking the Golden Rule to a higher and more focused level, we recommend you follow the wisdom of noted author, professional speaker and fellow member of The National Speakers Association Tony Alessandra, Ph.D., as stated in his best selling book, *The Platinum Rule*, *"Do unto others the way they want to be done unto"* You will never go wrong and you may gain a lifetime of friendship and loyalty.

I wish you the very best success with all of your new home customers, regardless of what culture, country... or planet they may come from.

---Michael D. Lee
Castro Valley, CA

RESOURCES

In addition to hundreds of interviews with new home salespeople, builders, developers and customers the following are some of the resources used in the development of this book:

Abdrabbah, B. (1984). *Saudi Arabia: Forces of Modernism.* Brattleboro, VT: Amana Books.

Ahmed, L. (1992). *Women and Gender in Islam.* New Haven, CT: Yale University.

Alessandra, T. (1996). *The Platinum Rule.* New York, NY: Warner Books, Inc.

Alier, A. (1990). *The Southern Sudan: Too many agreements dishonored.* Exeter, UK: Ithaca.

Allport, G.W. *The Nature of Prejudice.* Boston: Addison-Wesley Publishing Company.

Almaney, A.J. (1982). *Communicating with the Arabs.* Prospect Heights, IL: Waveland Press.

Amand, R.P. (Ed.).(1981). *Cultural Factors in International Relations.* New Delhi: Abinhav.

Argyle, M. (1975). *Bodily Communication.* London: Methuen.

Argyle, M. & Cook, M. (1976). *Gaze and Mutual Gaze.* England: Cambridge University Press.

Asante, M. & Newmark, E. (Eds.) *Handbook of Intercultural Communication.* Beverly Hills, CA: Sage Publications.

Asante, M.K. (1987). *The Afrocentric Idea.* Philadelphia: Temple University Press.

Asante, M.K. (1988). *Afrocentricity.* Trenton, NJ: Africa World Press.

Asante, M.K. (Ed.)(1985). *African Culture.* Westport, CT: Greenwood Press.

Asian American Handbook (1991). Chicago: National Conference on Christians and Jews, Asian American Journalists Association.

Axtell, R.E. (1990). *Do's and Taboos of Hosting International Visitors.* New York: John Wiley.

Axtell, R.E. (1991). *Gestures: The do's and taboos of body language around the world.* New York: John Wiley.

Axtell, R.E. (1994). *The do's and taboos of international trade.* New York: John Wiley.

Barth, F. (1969). *Ethnic Groups and Boundaries.* London: Allen and Unwin.

Beardsmore, H. (1992). *Bilingualism: Basic Principles.* London: Teitro, Ltd.

Bell, C. (1987). *The Unique Pacific.* London: The Centre for Security and Conflict Studies.

Benedict, R. (1934). *Patterns of Culture.* Boston: Houghton Mifflin.

Berger, C. & Chaffee, S. (Eds) (1987). *Handbook of Communication Science.* Newbury Park, CA: Sage.

Berlin, B. & Kay, P. (1969). *Basic Color Terms.* Berkeley, CA: University of California Press.

Berry, J., Dasen, P. & Saraswathi, T. (Eds.)(1997). *Handbook of Cross-Cultural Psychology.* Boston: Allyn & Bacon.

Beyer, S. (1974). *The Buddhist Experience.* Belmont, CA: Wadsworth.

Billingsley, A. (1974), *Black Families and the Struggle for Survival: Teaching our children to walk tall.* New York: Friendship Press.

Binh, D.T. (1975). *A Handbook for Teachers of Vietnamese Students: Hints for dealing with cultural differences in schools.* Arlington, VA: Center for Applied Linguistics.

Binnendijk, H. (Ed.).(1987). *National Negotiating Styles.* Washington, DC: Center for the Study of Foreign Affairs, U.S. Department of State.

Birke-Smith, K. (1959). *The Eskimos.* London: Methuen.

Blackbourn, D. & Evans, R.J. (Eds.)(1991). *The German Bourgeoisie.* London: Routledge.

Blaker, M.K. (1977). *Japanese International Negotiating Style.* New York: Columbia University Press.

Bloomfield, F. (1983). *The Book of Chinese Beliefs.* New York: Ballantine Books.

Bochner, S. (Ed.).(1981). *The Mediating Person: Bridges between cultures.* Boston: Hall.

Bosmajian, H.A. (1983). *The Language of Oppression.* Lanham, MD: University Press of America.

Braganti, N.L. & Devine, E. (1984). *The travelers' guide to European customs and manners.* Deephaven, MN: Meadowbrook.

Briggs, V.N. (1977). *The Chicano Worker.* Austin, TX: University of Texas Press.

Brigham Young University (1992). *Culturegrams.* Provo, UT: David M. Kennedy Center for International Studies.

Brislin, R. (1986). *Intercultural Interactions: A practical guide.* Beverly Hills, CA Sage.

Buell, L.H. (1984). *Understanding the Immigrant Cambodian.* San Diego: Los Amigos Research Associates.

Buell, L.H. (1984). *Understanding the Refugee Laotian.* San Diego: Los Amigos Research Associates.

Buell, L.H. (1984). *Understanding the Immigrant Mexican.* San Diego: Los Amigos Research Associates.

Buell, L.H. (1984). *Understanding the Refugee Chinese.* San Diego: Los Amigos Research Associates.

Buell, L.H. (1984). *Understanding the Refugee Vietnamese.* San Diego: Los Amigos Research Associates.

Buell, L.H. (1984). *Understanding the Immigrant Iraqi.* San Diego: Los Amigos Research Associates.

Burbidge, L.C. (1993). *The State of Black America.* New York: National Urban League.

Burgoon, J.K., et al. (1988). *Non-verbal Communication: The unspoken dialog.* New York: Harper & Row.

Butturff, D. & Epstein, E. (Eds.)(1978). *Women's Language and Styles.* Akron, OH: L&S Books.

Campbell, C.P. (1995). *Race, Myth and the News*. Thousand Oaks, CA: Sage.

Campbell, I.C. (1989). *A History of the Pacific Islands*. Berkeley: University of California Press.

Campbell, L.R. (1994). *Learning About Culturally Diverse Populations*. Asha. 36 (6/7).

Canda, E.R. & Phaobtong, T. (1992). Buddhism as a support system for Southeast Asian refugees. *Social Work*, 37(1).

Caplan, N., Whitmore, J.K. & Choy, M.H. (1989). *The Boat People and Achievement in America*. Ann Arbor, MI: The University of Michigan Press.

Carbaugh, D. (Ed.)(1990). *Cultural Communication and Intercultural Contact*. Hillsdale, NJ: Lawrence Erlbaum.

Cardona, G. (1992). Indo-Iranian languages. *International Encyclopedia of Linguistics, 2*. New York: Oxford University Press.

Carrasquillo, A. (1991). *Hispanic Children and Youth in the United States*. New York: Garland Publishing.

Carroll, R. (1988). *Cultural Misunderstanding: The French-American experience*. Chicago: University of Chicago Press.

Cashman, S.D. (1991). *African-Americans and the Quest for Civil Rights*. New York: New York University.

Casse, P. & Deol, S. (1985). *Managing Intercultural Negotiations*. Yarmouth, ME: Intercultural Press.

Chai, C. & Chai, W. (1965). *The Sacred Books of Confucius and Other Confucian Classics*. New York: Bantam Books.

Chambers, J.W. Jr. (1983). *Black English: Educational Equity and the Law*. Tucson: Karoma Publishers.

Chang, R. & Chang, M. (1992). *Speaking of Chinese*. New York: Oxford University Press.

Chang, S. (1991). *Asian Americans: An Interpretive History*. Boston: Twayne Publishers.

Cheng, L.L. & Ima, K. (1989). *Understanding the Immigrant Pacific Islander*. San Diego, Los Amigos Research Associates.

Choy, B. (1979). *Koreans in America*. Chicago: Nelson-Hall.

Chu, C. (1991). *The Asian Mind Game*. New York: Rawson Associates.

Cima, R. (Ed.)(1989). *Vietnam: A Country Study*. Washington, D.C.: United States Government as represented by the Secretary of the Army.

Clark, S. & Kelley, S. (1992). Traditional Native-American Values. *Journal of Rehabilitation*, 58(2).

Cleveland, H. (1960). *The Overseas Americans*. New York: McGraw-Hill.

Clifford, J. (1989). *The Predicament of Culture*. Cambridge, MA: Harvard University Press.

Cohen, R. (1991). *Negotiating Across Cultures: Communication obstacles in international diplomacy*. Washington, DC: U.S. Institute of Peace Press.

Condon, J. (1985). *Good Neighbors: Communicating with the Mexicans.* Yarmouth, ME: Intercultural Press.

Condon, J. & Yousef, F. (1975). *An Introduction to Intercultural Communication.* New York: Bobbs-Merrill.

Cordova, F. (1983). *Filipinos: Forgotten Asian Americans.* Dubuque, IA: Kendall/Hunt.

Costa, J.A. & Bomossy, G.J. (Eds.). *Marketing in a Multicultural World: Ethnicity, nationalism and cultural identity.* Thousand Oaks, CA: Sage.

Cox, T. (1993). *Cultural Diversity in Organizations.* San Francisco: Berrett-Koehler.

Dalton, B. (1992). *Indonesia.* Chicago: Passport Books.

Dance, F. (Ed.)(1982). *Human Communication Theory.* New York: Harper & Row.

Das, V. (Ed.)(1987). *Structure and Cognition: Aspects of Hindu caste and ritual.* Delhi: Oxford University Press.

De Bary, T. (1969). *The Buddhist Tradition in India, China, and Japan.* New York: Random House.

DeMente, B. (1989). *Korean Etiquette and Ethics in Business.* Lincolnwood, IL: NTC Publishing Group.

DeVito, J.A. (1986). *The Communication Handbook: A dictionary.* New York: Harper & Row.

DeVos, G. & Romanucci-Ross, L. (Eds.)(1975). *Ethnic Identity: Cultural continuities and change.* Palo Alto, CA: Mayfield.

Dillard, J.L. (1972). *Black English: Its History and Usage in the United States.* New York: Random House.

Dodge, E.S. (1976). *Islands and Empires: Western Impact on the Pacific and East Asia.* Minneapolis: University of Minnesota Press.

Dovidio, J. & Gaertner, S. (Eds.)(1986). *Prejudice, Discrimination, and Racism.* New York: Academic Press.

Downs, J. (1971). *Cultures in Crisis.* Chicago: Glencoe.

Dresser, N. (1996). *Multicultural Manners.* New York: John Wiley.

Dudden, A.P. (1992). *The American Pacific: From the Old China Trade to Present.* New York: Oxford University Press.

Durkheim, E. (1965). *The Elementary Forms of the Religious Life.* Glencoe, IL: Free Press.

Ebihara, M. (1966). Interrelations Between Buddhism and Social Systems in Cambodia Peasant Culture. *Anthropological Studies in Theravada Buddhism.* New Haven, CT: Yale University, Southeast Asian Studies.

Eitel, E.J. (1970). *Handbook of Chinese Buddhism.* Amsterdam: Philo Press.

Elias, N. (1982). *The History of Manners.* New York: Pantheon.

Engineer, A.A. (1992). *The Rights of Women in Islam.* New York: St. Martin's Press.

Epstein, A.L. (1987). *Ethos and Identity.* Chicago: Aldine.

Erez, M. & Earley, P.C. (1993). *Culture, Self-identity, and Work.* New York: Oxford University Press.

Erickson, J. (1979). *Islands of the South Pacific.* Menlo Park, CA: Lane Publishing Co.

Ethridge, J.M. (1990). *China's Unfinished Revolution.* San Francisco: China Books and Periodicals.

Europa Publications Limited (1994). *The Middle East and North Africa* (40th ed.) England: Staples Printers Rochester Limited.

Famighetti, R. (ed.)(1994). *The World Almanac and Book of Facts.* Mahwah, NJ: Funk & Wagnalls.

Farah, C.E. (1970). *Islam: Beliefs and Observances.* Barron's Educational Series. New York: Woodbury.

Farah, M. (1984). *Marriage and Sexuality in Islam.* Salt Lake City: University of Utah Press.

Featherstone, M. (1990). *Global Culture: Nationalism, globalization and modernity.* London: Sage.

Ferguson, H. (1987) *Manual for Multicultural Education.* Yarmouth, ME: Intercultural Press.

Fiatoa, L. & Palafox, N. (1980). *The Samoans.* Honolulu: The University of Hawaii, School of Medicine.

Fisher, B.A. (1978). *Perspectives on Human Communication.* New York: Macmillan.

Fisher, G. (1980). *International Negotiation: A Cross-Cultural Perspective.* Chicago, IL: Intercultural Press.

Fixico, D. L. (1986). *Termination and Relocation: Federal Indian Policy, 1945-1960.* Albuquerque, NM: University of New Mexico Press.

Forbes, J.D. (1977). *The Chicano Worker.* Austin, TX: University of Texas Press.

Frederick, H.H. (1993). *Global Communication and International Relations.* Belmont, CA: Wadsworth.

Furlonge, G. (1971). *Traditional Islamic Society.* In M. Adams (Ed.), *The Middle East: A Handbook.* England: Anthony Blond Ltd.

Furnham, A. & Bochnew, S. (1986). *Culture Shock: Psychological reactions to unfamiliar environments.* New York: Methuen.

Gall, S.B. & Gall, T.L. (1993). *Statistical Record of Asian Americans.* Detroit: Gale Research.

Gard, R.A. (1961). *Buddhism.* New York: George Braziller.

Gardwood, A.N. (Ed.)(1993). *Hispanic Americans: A Statistical Sourcebook.* Boulder, CO: Numbers & Concepts.

Garreau, J. (1981). *The Nine Nations of North America.* New York: Houghton Mifflin.

Geddes, R.W. (1976). *Migrants of the Mountains: The cultural ecology of the Blue Miau (Hmong) of Thailand.* Oxford, England: Clarendon.

Geertz, C. (1973). *The Interpretation of Cultures.* New York: Basic Books.

Glazer, N. & Moynihan, D. (1963). *Beyond the Melting Pot.* Cambridge: MIT Press & Harvard University Press.

Glazer, N. & Moynihan, D. (1975). *Ethnicity: Theory and Experience.* Cambridge, MA: Harvard University Press.

Gochenour, T. (1990). *Considering Filipinos.* Yarmouth, ME: Intercultural Press.

Gorden, M. (1964). *Assimilation in American Life.* Oxford, UK: Oxford University Press.

Gray, P. (1991). Whose America? *TIME Magazine,* 7/8 issue, 12-20.

Grebler, L., et al. (1970). *The Mexican American People.* New York: Free Press.

Greene, M. (1993). *The Passions of Pluralism: Multiculturalism and the Expanding Community.* Educational Researcher, 22(1), 13-18.

Gronbeck, G., Farrell, T. & Soukup, P. (Eds.).(1991). *Media, Consciousness, and Culture.* Newbury Park, CA: Sage.

Grossier, P.L. (1982). *The United States and the Middle East.* Albany, NY: State University of New York Press.

Gudykunst, W. (1984). *Communicating with Strangers: An approach to intercultural communication.* Reading, MA: Addison-Wesley.

Gudykunst, W. (1989). *Theories in Intercultural Communication.* Newbury Park, CA: Sage.

Gudykunst, W. (1998). *Bridging Differences: Effective Intergroup Communication.* Thousand Oaks, CA: Sage.

Guernica, A. (1982). *Reaching the Hispanic market effectively.* New York: McGraw-Hill.

Gulliver, P.H. (1979). *Disputes and Negotiations: A cross-cultural perspective.* New York: Academic Press.

Gutmann, A. (Ed.)(1992). *Multiculturalism and the Politics of Recognition.* Princeton, NJ: Princeton University Press.

Hall, E.T. (1977). *Beyond Culture.* New York: Anchor Books.

Hall, E.T. (1981). *The Silent Language.* New York: Doubleday.

Hall, E.T. (1982). *The Hidden Dimension.* New York: Doubleday.

Hall, J. & Beadsley, R. (1965). *Twelve Doors to Japan.* New York: McGraw-Hill.

Harris, P.R. & Morgan, R.T. (1991). *Managing Cultural Differences.* Houston, Gulf.

Hayakawa, S.I. (1978). *Through the Communication Barrier.* New York: Harper & Row.

Hayes-Bautista, D.E. (1992). *No Longer A Minority: Latinos and Social Policy in California.* Los Angeles: Chicano Studies Research Center, University of California.

Hecht, M.L. (1993). *African American Communication.* Thousand Oaks, CA: Sage.

Heider, F. (1958). *The Psychology of Interpersonal Relations.* New York: John Wiley.

Henry, W.A. (1990). *Beyond the Melting Pot.* Time Magazine, 135(15), 28-31.

Glenn, E.S., Witmeyer, D. & Stevenson, K. (1977). Cultural Styles of Persuasion. *International Journal of Intercultural Relations,* I(3), 52-66.

Hinnells, J.R. (1997). *Dictionary of Religions.* London: Penguin Books.

Hobday, P. (1978) *Saudi Arabia Today.* New York: St. Martin's Press.

Hofstede, G. (1980). *Culture's Consequences.* Newbury Park, CA: Sage.

Hollinger, D.A. (1995). *Post-ethnic America: Beyond multiculturalism.* New York: Basic Books.

Horowitz, D.L. (1985). *Ethnic Groups in Conflict.* Berkeley, University of California Press.

Horton, C.P. & Smith, J.C. (Eds.)(1993). *Statistical Record of Black America.* (2nd ed.). Detroit: Gale Research.

Hsu, F.L. (1963). *Caste, Clan and Club.* Princeton, NJ: Van Nostrand.

Hsu, F.L. (1981). *American and Chinese: Passage to differences.* Honolulu, University of Hawaii Press.

Hurh, W.M. & Kwang, C.K. (1984). *Korean Immigrants in America.* Cranbury, NJ: Fairleigh Dickinson University Press.

Ikle, F.C. (1987). *How Nations Negotiate.* New York: Harper & Row.

Imai, M. (1981). *Sixteen Ways to Avoid Saying No.* Tokyo: Nihon Keizai Shimbun.

Ingrams, D. (1971). *The Position of Women in Middle East Arab Society.* In M. Adams (Ed.), *The Middle East: A Handbook.* England: Anthony Blond Ltd.

Isaacs, J. (1980). *Australian Dreaming: 40,000 years of aboriginal history.* Sydney: Lansdowne.

Jandt, F.E. (1998). *Intercultural Communication: An introduction.* Thousand Oaks, CA: Sage.

Johnstone, P. (1993) *Operation World.* Harrisonburg, VA: R.R. Donnelly & Sons.

Jones, S. (1993). *The Right Touch: Understanding and using the language of physical contact.* Cresskill, NJ: Hampton Press.

Joy, A. (1989). *Ethnicity in Canada.* New York: AMS.

Katriel, T. (1986). *Talking Straight: Dugri Speech in Israeli Sabra Culture.* England: Cambridge University Press.

Keesing, R.M. (1988). *Melanesian Pidgin and the Oceanic Substrate.* Stanford, CA: Stanford University Press.

Khuri, F. (1968, August). The etiquette of bargaining in the Middle East. *American Anthropologist, 4,* 698-706.

Kim, H. (1985). *Facts About Korea.* (18th Ed.). Seoul, Korea: Samhwa Publishing Company.

Kim, Y.Y. (1986). *Interethnic Communication: Current research.* Newbury Park, CA: Sage.

Kim, Y.Y. (1988). *Cross-cultural Adaptation: Current approaches.* Newbury Park, CA: Sage.

Kincaid, D.L. (Ed.)(1987). *Communication Theory: Eastern and Western Perspectives.* New York: Academic Press.

Kitano, H. (1976) *Japanese Americans.* Englewood Cliffs, NJ: Prentice-Hall.

Kitayama, S. & Markus, H.(Eds.)(1994). *Culture, Self, and Emotions.* Washington, DC: American Psychological Association.

Kleg, M. (1993). *Hate, Prejudice, and Racism.* Albany: State University of New York Press.

Kluckhohn, F. & Strodtbeck, F. (1961). *Variations in Value Orientations.* New York: Row, Peterson.

Kochman, T. (1981). *Black & White Styles in Conflict.* Chicago: The University of Chicago Press.

Kohls, R.L. (1988). *The Values Americans Live By.* San Francisco: LinguaTec.

Koller, J.M. (1982). *The Indian Way.* New York: Macmillan.

Korean Overseas Information Service. (1986). *Focus on Korea.* Korea: Samsung Moonwha Printing Company.

Korzenny, F. & Ting-Toomey, S. (Eds.).(1990). *Communicating For Peace: Diplomacy and negotiation.* Newbury Park, CA: Sage.

Kozlowski, G.C. (1991). *The Concise History of Islam and the Origin of its Empires.* Acton, MA: Copley Publishing Group.

Kremenyuk, V.A. (Ed.).(1991). *International Negotiation: Analysis, approaches, issues.* San Francisco: Jossey-Bass.

Kroeber, a. & Kluckhohn, C. (1963). *Culture: A critical review of concepts and definitions.* New York: Random House.

Labov, W. (1972). *Language in the Inner City: Studies in the Black English Vernacular.* Philadelphia: University of Philadelphia Press.

Landis, D. & Boucher, J. (1987). *Ethnic Conflict.* Newbury Park, CA: Sage.

Landis, D. & Brislin (Eds.)(1983). *Handbook of Intercultural Training.* Elmsford, NY: Pergamon.

Latino Legislative Caucus Hearings. (1991). *Latinos at a Crossroads: Challenges and Opportunities into the 21st Century.* California: Latino Legislative Caucus Hearings.

Lazarus, R. (1991). *Emotion and Adaptation.* New York: Oxford University Press.

Lebra, T.S. (1976). *Japanese Patterns of Behavior.* Honolulu: The University Press of Hawaii.

Leone, B. (1992). *Native Languages and Cultures.* Bilingual Basics, Summer/Fall 1992.

Levine, R.A. & Campbell, D.T.(1972). *Ethnocentrism: Theories of conflict, ethnic attitudes and group behavior.* New York: John Wiley

Li, C.N. (1992). *International Encyclopedia of Linguistics.* New York: Oxford University Press.

Locke, D. (1992). *Increasing Multicultural Understanding.* Newbury Park, CA: Sage.

Long, S.O. (1992). *Japan: A Country Study.* Washington, D.C.: Department of the Army.

Lopreato, J. (1970). *Italian Americans.* New York: Random House.

Luce, D. & Sommer, J. (1969). *Viet Nam - The Unheard Voices.* Ithica, NY: Cornell University Press.

Mackie, D. & Hamilton, D.(Eds.)(1993). *Affect, Cognition, and Stereotyping.* San Diego, CA: Academic Press.

Macrae, C., Stangor, C. & Hewstone, M. (Eds.) *Stereotypes and Stereotyping.* New York: Guilford.

Magnetti, D. & Sigler, M. (1973). *An Introduction to the Near East.* Huntington, IN: Our Sunday Visitor.

Major, J.S. (1989). *The Land and People of China.* New York: J.B. Lippincott.

Marin, G. & Marin, B. (1991). *Research With Hispanic Populations.* Beverly Hills, CA: Sage Publications.

Matics, M.L. (1970). *Entering the Path of Enlightenment.* New York: Macmillan.

Mautner-Markhof, F. (Ed.). *Processes of International Negotiations.* Boulder, CO: Westview.

May, L. & Sharratt, S.C. (1994). *Applied Ethics: A multicultural approach.* Englewood Cliffs, NJ: Prentice Hall.

McAdoo, H.P. & McAdoo, J.L. (Eds.). (1985). *Black Children.* Beverly Hills, CA Sage Publications.

McNaughton, W. (1974). *The Confucian Vision.* Ann Arbor: University of Michigan Press.

McWillians, C. (1990). *North from Mexico.* New York: Greenwood Press.

Mehrrabian, A. (1981). *Silent Messages: Implicit communication of emotions and attitudes.* Belmont, CA: Wadsworth.

Meier, F. (1971). *Islam and its Cultural Divergence.* Urbana, IL: University of Illinois Press.

Melendex, E (1991). *Hispanics in the Labor Force: Issues and Policies.* New York: Plenum Press.

Menez, H.Q. (1980). *Folklore Communication Among Filipinos in America.* New York: Arno Press.

Metz, H.C. (Ed.). (1990). *Iraq: A Country Study.* Washington, D.C.: Federal Research Division, Library of Congress. Headquarters, Dept. of the Army.

Miller, G. & Steinberg, M. (1975). *Between People.* Chicago: Science Research Associates.

Min, P.G. (Ed.)(1995). *Asian Americans: Contemporary Trends and Issues.* Thousand Oaks, CA: Sage.

Moran, R. & Stripp, W. (1991). *Successful International Business Negotiations.* Houston: Gulf.

Morris, D. (1979). *Gestures: Their Origins and Distribution.* London: Cape.

Morris, D. (1995). *Bodytalk: The meaning of human gestures.* New York: Crown Trade Paperbacks.

Mosher, S.W. (1983). *Broken Earth: The Rural Chinese.* New York: The Free Press.

Nakamura, H. (1964). *Ways of Thinking of Eastern Peoples.* Honolulu: East-West Center Press.

Nakane, C. (1970). *Japanese Society.* Berkeley: University of California Press.

Namamura, N. (1988). *Nippon: The Land and its People.* Japan: Gakuseisha Publishing.

Nash, J.C. (1966). *Anthropological Studies in Theravada Buddhism.* New Haven, CT: Yale University Southeast Asia Studies

Nicolau, S. & S. Santiestevan, S. (Eds.). (1990). *The Hispanic Almanac.* New York: Hispanic Policy Development Project.

Nyrop, R.F. (Ed.)(1982). *Federal Republic of Germany, A Country Study.* Washington, DC: U.S. Government Printing Office.

Oey, T. (1993). *Everyday Indonesian.* Chicago: Passport Books.

Omi, M. & Winant, H. (1986). *Racial Group Formation in the United States.* New York: Routledge.

Padilly, A.M. (Ed.)(1980). *Acculturation: Theory, models and some new findings.* Boulder, CO: Westview.

Padilla, A.M. (Ed.)(1995). *Hispanic Psychology.* Thousand Oaks, CA: Sage.

Park, R. (Ed.)(1950). *Race and Culture.* New York: Free Press.

Pedersen, P. (1988). *A Handbook to Develop Multicultural Awareness.* Washington, DC: AACD.

Penfield, J. (1990). *Understanding Asian Americans.* New York: Neal-Schuman Publishers.

Phillips, S. (1982). *The Invisible Culture.* New York: Longman.

Ponterotto, J.G. & Pedersen, P.B. (1993). *Preventing Prejudice.* Thousand Oaks, CA: Sage.

Portes, A. & Rumbaut, R. (1990). *Immigrant America: A Portrait.* Berkeley, CA: University of California Press.

Posses, F. (1978). *The Art of International Negotiation.* London: Business Press.

Prosser, M.H. (1978). *The Cultural Dialogue: An introduction to intercultural communication.* Boston: Houghton Mifflin.

Pye, L. (1982). *Chinese Commercial Negotiating Style.* Cambridge, MA: Oelgeschlager, Gunn & Hain.

Radhakrishnan, S. (1979). *Indian Religions.* New Delhi: Vision Books.

Reischauer, E. (1977). *The Japanese.* Cambridge, MA: Harvard University Press.

Rodinson, M. (1981). *The Arabs.* London: Croom Helm.

Rokeach, M. (1972). *Beliefs, Attitudes, and Values.* San Francisco: Jossey-Bass.

Roosens, E. (1989). *Creating Ethnicity: The process of ethnogenesis.* Newbury Park, CA Sage.

Root, M. (Ed.)(1995). *The Multiracial Experience.* Thousand Oaks, CA: Sage.

Rossman, M.L. (1994). *Multicultural marketing: Selling to a diverse America.* New York: Amacom.

Rothenberg, P.S. (Ed.)(1992). *Race, Class and Gender in the United States.* New York: St. Martin's.

Rothman, J. (1992). *From Confrontation to Cooperation: Resolving ethnic and regional conflict.* Newbury Park, CA: Sage.

Saitz, R.I. (1972). *Handbook of Gestures: Colombia and the United States.* The Hague: Mouton.

Salacuse, J. (1991). *Making Global Deals: Negotiating in the international market place.* Boston: Houghton Mifflin.

Samovar, L.A. (1981). *Understanding Intercultural Communication.* Belmont, CA: Wadsworth.

Samovar, L.A. & Porter, R.E. (Eds.) *Intercultural Communication: A reader.* Belmont, CA: Wadsworth.

Sarbaugh, L.E. (1979). *Intercultural Communication.* Rochelle Park, NJ: Hayden Book Company.

Schultz, B. (1998). *Smart Selling Techniques.* Boca Raton, FL: New Home Specialist.

Schultz, B. (1997). *The Official Handbook for New Home Salespeople.* Boca Raton, FL: New Home Specialist.

Segall, M.H. (1966). *The influence of culture on visual perception.* Indianapolis: Bobbs-Merrill.

Shack, W. & Skinner, E. (1979). *Strangers in African Societies.* Berkeley: University of California Press.

Sharma, I.C. (1965). *Ethical philosophies of India.* New York: Harper & Row.

Shelley, R. (1993). *Culture Shock: A Guide to Customs and Etiquette of Japan.* Portland, OR: Graphic Arts Center Publishing Company.

Shorris, E. (1992). *Latinos.* New York: W.W. Norton Company.

Singer, M. (1987). *Intercultural Communication: A perceptual approach.* Englewood Cliffs, NJ: Prentice-Hall.

Sitaram, K.S. & Cogdell, R.T. (1976). *Foundations of Intercultural Communication.* Columbus, OH: Merrill.

Smith, A. (1986). *The Ethnic Origins of Nations.* Oxford, UK: Basil Blackwell.

Sreenivasa Murthy, H.V. (1973). *Studies in Indian Culture.* Bombay: Asia Publishing House.

Stern, J. (1989). *The Filipino Americans.* New York: Chelsea House Publishers.

Stewart, E. (1972). *American Cultural Patterns: A cross-cultural perspective.* Yarmouth, ME: Intercultural Press.

Stryk, L. (1968). *World of the Buddha: A reader – from the three baskets to modern Zen.* New York: Doubleday.

Takaki, R. (1993). *A Different Mirror: A History of Multicultural America.* Boston: Little, Brown.

Thomas, R. (1991). *Beyond Race & Gender.* New York: AMACOM.

Tidwell, B.J. (1993). *The State of Black America 1993.* New York: National Urban League.

Triandis, H.C. (1994). *Culture and Social Behavior.* New York: McGraw-Hill.

Trilling, L. (1968). *Beyond Culture.* New York: Viking.

Tsujimura, A. (1968). *Japanese Culture and Communication.* Tokyo: NHK Books.

Veltman, C. (1988). *The Future of the Spanish Language in the United States.* New York: Hispanic Policy Development Project.

Wadley, S. & Jacobson, D. (Eds.)(1977). *Women in India: Two perspectives.* New Delhi: Manohar.

Watson, O.M. (1970). *Proxemic Behavior: A Cross-cultural Study.* The Hague: Mouton.

Weiss, S.E. & Stripp, W. (1985). *Negotiating With Foreign Persons.* New York: New York University Press.

West, C. (1993). *Race Matters.* Boston: Beacon Press.

Williams, R. (1976). *Keywords: A vocabulary of culture and society. London: Fontana.*

Williams, R. (1981). *Culture.* London: Fontana.

Wilson, C.C. & Gutierrez, F. (1995). *Race, Multiculturalism, and the Media.* Thousand Oaks, CA: Sage.

Wiseman, R. & Koester, J. (Eds.)(1993). *Intercultural Communication Competence.* Newbury Park, CA: Sage.

Wong, A.M. (1993). *Target: The U.S. Asian Market – A practical guide to doing business.* Palos Verdes, CA: Pacific Heritage Books.

Woodson, C.G. (1968). *The African Background Outlined.* New York: Negro Universities Press.

Wright, A.F. (1962). *Confucian Personalities.* Stanford, CA: Stanford University Press.

Wright, G. (1981). *Building the Dream: A social history of housing in America.* New York: Pantheon.

Yee, A. H. (1984). *A Search For Meaning: Essays of a Chinese American.* San Francisco: Chinese Historical Society of America.

Yinger, M. (1994). *Ethnicity.* Albany: State University of New York Press.

Young, B. (1980). *People and Cultures of Hawaii.* Honolulu, University of Hawaii.

Young, K. (1968). *Negotiating with the Chinese Communists.* New York: McGraw-Hill.

Zarembka, A. (1990). *The Urban Housing Crisis.* New York: Greenwood Press.

Zelinsky, W. (1973). The Cultural Geography of the United States. Englewood Cliffs, NJ: Prentice Hall.

Zimmerman, M. (1985). *How To Do Business with the Japanese.* New York: Random House.

APPENDIX: CULTURAL CUE CARDS

The following are general characteristics of cultural groups that can vary widely from individual to individual within a particular culture. These are not intended to be used to stereotype your customers, but are meant to serve as a guide to understanding different cultures, help develop rapport and assist you in meeting your customer's needs.

CHARACTERISTICS TYPICAL OF MOST AMERICANS

Meeting and Greeting
♦ Are very informal people
♦ Will shake hands enthusiastically; may even pat people on the back

Eye Contact
♦ Strong eye contact
♦ Take it as a sign of honesty & integrity

Personal Space
♦ Shake hands and then drop them
♦ Like to maintain a distance of about 1.5 to 2.5 feet

Negotiating
♦ Are not used to negotiating
♦ Tend to have a "take it or leave it" attitude

♦ Focus on the commodity being negotiated
♦ Don't do much small talk before getting down to business

Communications
♦ Tend to be open; will say what's on their minds

TYPICAL AMERICAN CHARACTERISTICS (continued)

Beliefs
- Believe the following are good luck symbols:
  Rabbit's foot
  Horse shoe
  The number 7
- Believe the following are bad luck symbols:
  Black cats
  Walking under ladders
  The numbers 13 and 666

Gestures
- Are very demonstrative
- Show the OK sign to mean "all right"
- Often point with index finger

Posture
- Generally very relaxed
- Leaning is common

Walking Pace
- Is Fast

Demonstrating Emotions in Public
- Demonstrative

Use of First Names
- Prefer using first names as quickly as possible
- Older people should not be called by first name until they invite you to do so

Business Cards
- Not automatically exchanged
- Commonly write information on the back
- Are generally very careless with cards

Punctuality
- Consider no more than 15 minutes late acceptable
- Believe that "time is money"

OTHER MULTICULTURAL GROUPS

The most prevalent groups coming into the United States today are Hispanic, Asian, Southeast Asian and Middle Eastern. These are the groups having the biggest impact on the new home industry right now.

HISPANICS

Meeting and Greeting
- May hug members of the same sex, called "abrazo"
- The longer the hug, the deeper the friendship

Eye Contact
- Strong eye contact
- May drop eyes as a sign of respect
- Don't give long eye contact to members of the opposite sex – can seem flirtatious

Personal Space
- 1 to 2 feet

Negotiating
- Are very good negotiators
- Start very slow and low priced
- Build a relationship, which is more important than the commodity being negotiated

Communication
- Are very open between acquaintances

Beliefs
- Similar to those of other Americans
- Mexicans observe "Day of the Dead," a popular annual holiday to honor their ancestors. (Coincides with the Christian celebrations of All Saints' Day and All Souls' Day, Nov. 1&2)

Posture
- Relaxed

Walking Pace
- Slow paced

HISPANICS (continued)

Displaying Emotions in Public
♦ Very demonstrative

Use of First Names
♦ Rarely used except among close friends
♦ May call you by last name
♦ Name and titles are important

Business Cards
♦ Are given at start of business meetings

Punctuality
♦ Up to 30 minutes late is considered acceptable
♦ Social events always start late

ASIANS

Meeting and Greeting
Chinese:
♦ Will bow to each other in China
♦ Here will often shake hands while bowing head slightly

Japanese:
♦ Are very ritualistic
♦ Will bow to each other in Japan
♦ The lower the bow, the deeper the respect

Koreans:
♦ Will bow to each other in Korea

Southeast Asians:
♦ Will bow to each other in Southeast Asia

Filipinos:
♦ Usually shake hands

Eye Contact, Asians
♦ May avoid eye contact as a sign of respect

Personal Space
Chinese:
♦ Is very small due to crowded conditions in China, 1 to 2 feet

Japanese:
♦ Will shake hands or bow and then step back, 3 to 5 feet
♦ Are very formal people

Koreans:
♦ 2 to 3 feet

Southeast Asians:
♦ 2 to 3 feet

Filipinos:
♦ 1 to 2 feet

Negotiating
Chinese:
♦ Are tough negotiators
♦ Start embarrassingly low
♦ Are emotionally involved in the transaction
♦ Focus on relationships

ASIANS (continued)

Negotiating, continued
Japanese:
♦ Take forever to start negotiating
♦ Want to get to know the other party first
♦ Silence is crucial for thinking
♦ Focus on relationships
♦ Never say "no," but you should not assume agreement

Koreans:
♦ Are very aggressive and emotional in negotiations
♦ May yell or cry
♦ Focus on relationships

Southeast Asians:
♦ Are sharp negotiators
♦ Focus on relationships

Filipinos:
♦ Are good negotiators
♦ Can be quite emotional during negotiations

Communication, All Asians
♦ Are very closed in public
♦ Consider many subjects taboo

Beliefs
Chinese:
♦ Believe in "Feng Shui"
♦ Believe the following are good luck symbols: the color red, the number 8
♦ Believe that the following are bad luck symbols: the color white, the number 4

Japanese:
♦ Believe the following are good luck symbols: the color red, the number 8
♦ Believe the following are bad luck symbols: the color white, the number 4

Koreans:
♦ Believe the number 8 is a good luck symbol.
♦ Believe the following are bad luck symbols: the color red, the number 4
♦ Believe trees are sacred

Southeast Asians:
♦ Believe the number 8 is a good luck symbol.
♦ Believe the number 3 is a bad luck symbol.

ASIANS (continued)

Beliefs, continued
Filipinos:
♦ Believe the number 7 is a good luck symbol.
♦ Believe the number 3 is a bad luck symbol.

Gestures, Asians
♦ Use very little body language
♦ Point with entire hand

Posture, Asians
♦ Are very formal
♦ Tend to prefer feet flat on the floor

Walking Pace, Asians
♦ Fast but not as fast as Americans

Demonstrating Emotions in Public, Asians
♦ Are very restrained – to do so is almost taboo

Use of First Names, Asians
♦ Ask: "Which is your family name?"
♦ Don't use unless invited to do so
♦ Can be insulting, especially for older Asians

Use of First Names, specific Asian groups
Chinese:
♦ Rarely use first names
Japanese:
♦ Almost never use first names
♦ Call each other "San" preceded by family name, meaning Mr., Mrs. or Ms.
Koreans:
♦ Rarely use first names
Southeast Asians:
♦ Last name is often the first name
Filipinos:
♦ Commonly use first names with friends

Business cards, Asians
♦ Present with both hands, writing facing them
♦ Accept their card with your right
♦ Never write on the business card
♦ Never ask for another
♦ Exchanging cards is especially important in the Japanese culture (called "meishi")

ASIANS (continued)

<u>Punctuality, Asians</u>
- Up to 30 minutes late is considered acceptable
- Social events always start late

MIDDLE EASTERNERS

Meeting and Greeting
♦ Salaam is common – sweeping motion from heart to head

Eye Contact
♦ Very strong eye contact
♦ Degree of eye contact may be uncomfortable for most Americans
♦ Believe "The eyes are the windows to the soul"

Personal Space
♦ Very close, .5 to 1 feet

Negotiating
♦ Are very aggressive negotiators
♦ Are very emotional
♦ Can be intimidating

Communication
♦ Believe in saying what's on their minds
♦ Are very exaggerated

Beliefs
♦ The East is sacred

Gestures
♦ Are very demonstrative
♦ Do not eat or write with left hand

Posture
♦ Pointing bottom of foot at others is the highest insult possible

Walking Pace
♦ Quick

Displaying Emotions in Public
♦ Very demonstrative

Use of first names
♦ Is common, but wait until invited

Business cards
♦ Present with both hands, writing facing them
♦ Accept their card with your right hand and read it

Punctuality
♦ Up to 45 minutes late is considered acceptable
♦ Social events always start late

AFRICAN AMERICANS

Meeting and Greeting
- Can be very ritualistic
- Shake hands, then clasp finger, etc.

Eye Contact
- Strong eye contact when speaking, less when listening

Personal Space
- A little smaller space than most Americans are comfortable with, about 1.5 to 2 feet

Negotiating
- Older African Americans do not negotiate much
- Negotiating habits are very "Americanized"
- Younger African American's are pretty adept negotiators
- Tend to focus on the commodity being negotiated
- Can get quite emotional during negotiations

Communication
- Are very open between friends

- Are somewhat distrustful of outsiders

Beliefs
- Are very similar to most other Americans

Gestures
- Very, very demonstrative and animated

Posture
- Relaxed

Walking Pace
- Slower than most other Americans, but with style

Demonstrating Emotions in Public
- Very demonstrative

Use of First Names
- Don't use until after you get permission
- Can have very unique given names

Business Cards
- Not automatically exchanged
- Commonly write information on the back

AFRICAN AMERICANS (continued)

Business Cards (continued)

♦ Like most other Americans, can be generally careless with cards

Punctuality

♦ Can be a little less punctual than some other Americans

NATIVE AMERICANS

Meeting and Greeting
- Can be very formal with strangers
- Can be very familiar with friends

Eye Contact
- Strong eye contact when speaking
- May lower eyes when listening

Personal Space
- A little farther than common with strangers (2-3 feet)
- A little closer than common with friends (1-2 feet)

Negotiating
- Are usually pretty shrewd negotiators
- Are very concerned about the feelings of others during negotiation

Communication
- Are very open between friends
- Are very distrustful of outsiders

Beliefs
- Have a high respect for nature and the land
- Often do not believe that people should own land, just use it

Gestures
- Very demonstrative and animated

Posture
- Somewhat formal

Walking Pace
- Slower than European Americans

Demonstrating Emotions in Public
- Very demonstrative

Use of First Name
- Don't use until after you get permission
- The meaning of names is very important

Business Cards
- Not automatically exchanged

Punctuality
- Will often be half an hour late or more

ASIAN INDIANS

Meeting and Greeting
- Namaste is hands in prayer position in front of chest with a bow

Eye Contact
- May drop eyes as a sign of respect

Personal Space
- 2 to 3 feet

Negotiating
- Are tough negotiators

Communication
- Very restrained in public

Beliefs
- Vastu Shastra – brings good luck if you follow its rules

Demonstrating Emotions in Public
- Very restrained

Use of the first name
- Prefer titles

Business Cards
- Customarily exchange business cards

Punctuality
- Up to 30 minutes late is considered acceptable

EUROPEANS

Meeting and Greeting
English:
♦ Are formal people – shake hands

French:
♦ Use a light handshake

Germans:
♦ Use a firm handshake with only one pump

Italians:
♦ Hug, kiss cheeks

Eye Contact
English:
♦ Strong eye contact

French:
♦ Strong eye contact

Germans:
♦ Strong eye contact

Italians:
♦ Strong eye contact

Personal Space
Germans:
♦ Will step back after greeting
♦ 3 to 4 feet

French:
♦ Will step back after greeting
♦ 2.5 to 3.5 feet

English:
♦ Will stand their ground after greeting
♦ 2.5 to 3.5 feet

Italians:
♦ Will step in after greeting
♦ 1 to 2 feet

Negotiating
English:
♦ Are gentle but firm

French:
♦ Are gentle but firm

Germans:
♦ Are very firm and businesslike

EUROPEANS (continued)

Negotiating, continued
Italians:
- Are gentle but firm

Posture, Europeans
- Other than Italian, somewhat more formal than Americans

Walking Pace, Europeans
- English walk briskly

Displaying Emotion in Public
English:
- Very restrained

French:
- Somewhat demonstrative

Germans:
- Very restrained

Italians:
- Very demonstrative

Use of First Names
English:
- Use titles and last names

French:
- Prefer first names after they get to know you

Use of First Names, cont.
Germans:
- Almost never use first names
- Prefer titles and last names

Italians:
- Prefer first names

Business Cards, Europeans
Customarily exchange business cards

Punctuality, Europeans
- Most are very punctual
- Up to 15 minutes late is considered acceptable
- Germans are extremely punctual – do not be even one minute late!

CARIBBEAN ISLANDERS

Meeting and Greeting
♦ Are very informal people
♦ Will shake hands enthusiastically, may even pat people on the back or hug

Eye Contact
♦ Strong eye contact
♦ Take it as a sign of honesty & integrity

Personal Space
♦ Very intimate; .5 to 1.5 feet
♦ Often touch each other while talking

Negotiating
♦ Are very sharp negotiators
♦ Can be quite emotional during negotiations

Communications
♦ Open - will say what's on their minds
♦ Do not like to say, "No"
♦ Often say, "No problem," but this does not mean "Yes"

Beliefs
♦ Some believe in voodoo and black magic
♦ Most won't discuss it

Gestures
♦ Very demonstrative

Posture
♦ Very relaxed
♦ Leaning is common

Walking Pace
♦ Very slow and graceful, almost rhythmic movement when walking

Demonstrating Emotions in Public
♦ Very demonstrative

Use of First Names
♦ Prefer using first names as quickly as possible
♦ Older people should not be called by first names until invited
♦ Often have "nick names"

CARIBBEAN ISLANDERS (continued)

<u>Business Cards</u>
- Not automatically exchanged
- Most people do not have business cards; Only top officials have them

<u>Punctuality</u>
- Are very relaxed about time
- Can be as much as two hours late or more
- Believe that "life is for living"

NEW HOME SPECIALIST℠ PUBLISHING GROUP
Join other new homes sales professionals who are benefiting
from The Official New Home Sales Development System®

TITLE	QUANTITY	UNIT PRICE	TOTAL
The Official Handbook for New Home Salespeople by Bob Schultz		$ 34.95*	$
Smart Selling℠ Techniques by Bob Schultz		$ 34.95*	$
Selling to Multicultural Customers: The Official Guide for New Home Salespeople, by Michael Lee		$ 34.95*	
The Five Minute Professional - a 9-Tape Audio Cassette System by Bob Schultz		$ 125.00*	$
Smart Start℠ by Marilyn McVay		$ 99.95**	$
The Official New Home Sales Development System® Video, Volume 1 by Bob Schultz		$ 1,495.00***	$
The Official System for New Home Sales Follow-Through® by Steve Hoffacker		$ 695.00****	$
The Official System for New Home Sales Consumer Research℠ by Steve Hoffacker		$ 695.00****	$
Management System Reports (Computer Diskettes in Excel '97 Format) *Sales Performance Analysis* - Measure the Effectiveness of Each Salesperson		$ 99.95*	$
Marketing & Sales Cost Efficiency Analysis - Measure the Effectiveness of Your Marketing Dollars		$ 99.95*	$
SPECIAL! BOTH SYSTEMS FOR JUST		$ 159.95*	$

METHOD OF PAYMENT (US Funds Only)		
❏ Enclosed check made payable to New Home Specialist Inc.	TOTAL OF ITEMS ORDERED	$
	FL Residents, please add 6% sales tax	$
	*Shipping & Handling: $5.95 for first item; $3.75 for each add'l item	$
❏ Please charge my: American Express / Visa / MasterCard (Please circle one)	**Shipping & Handling: $9.95 for first item; $5.00 for each add'l item	
	***Shipping & Handling: $14.50 for each Video System	$
Account #:_____	****Shipping & Handling: $12.95 for first item; $7.00 for each add'l item	$
Expiration Date:_____	All shipping via UPS Groundtrack. For International or Federal Express, please call for shipping charges.	$
Signature:_____ (Required for all charge orders)		
	TOTAL	$

Date:_____

Name:_____

Company:_____

Address:_____

City:_____State:_____Zip:_____

Phone: (   )_____Fax:(   )_____

Email:_____

FAX YOUR ORDER - - (561) 368-1171. For phone orders or customer service, call (561) 368-1151.
Quantity discounts are available. Call for details or to discuss the following:

❏ Sales Seminars
❏ Strategic / Tactical Planning Retreats
❏ Adaptive Selling / Adaptive Management Reports

❏ Convention programs
❏ Comprehensive Sales / Management Consulting
❏ I'd like to receive - at no cost - your E-Mail Strategies Newsletter

❏ Smart Selling℠ & Smart Management Seminars featuring Bob Schultz

NEW HOME SPECIALIST ℠ EDUCATION SYSTEMS
2300 Glades Road ◆ Suite 330 W ◆ Boca Raton, Florida 33431 ◆ Phone: (561) 368-1151 ◆ Fax: (561) 368-1171
Email: newhomespec@emi.net ◆ Website: www.newhomespecialist.com

Prices subject to change without prior notification.

New Home Specialist^{SM} is dedicated to the new home sales profession. We are educators, trainers and consultants to hundreds of companies throughout North America and to thousands of new home sales professionals around the world.

Bob Schultz, MIRM, CSP, is the founder and president of New Home Specialist Inc. With Bob's extensive experience, and under his leadership, the company creates education and training systems that are unequaled in the industry. Our company publishes world-class resources such as books, management systems, video and audiocassette learning programs, which we are proud to offer as a part of *The Official New Home Sales Development System.*® Each is packed with powerful, effective and proven concepts, strategies, techniques and methods, that when applied, will accelerate you and your team along the road of personal and professional achievement.

If **YOU** would like access to the most recent live recorded presentations and articles containing current and insightful information by Michael Lee, Bob Schultz, or one of our other New Home Specialist associate consultants and facilitators, and to receive our bi-monthly *Strategies Newsletter* via e-mail, all on a complimentary basis, simply let us know who you are!

Print Name:_____

Title:_____

Company:_____

Address:_____

City:_____ State:_____ Zip Code:_____

Phone:_____ Fax:_____

Email:_____ Website:_____

Where and when did you acquire *Selling to Multicultural Customers: The Official Guide for New Home Salespeople*?_____

Please send to:
New Home Specialist Inc.
2300 Glades Road ◆ Suite 330 W
Boca Raton, Florida 33431

-or-

Call or fax:
Phone: (561) 368-1151
Fax: (561) 368-1171
Email: newhomespec@emi.net
Website: www.newhomespecialist.com